PENGUIN BUSINESS
DOGLAPAN

Indian businessman Ashneer Grover is the co-founder and former managing director of the Indian fintech company BharatPe. Grover is also a Shark (investor) on the reality TV show *Shark Tank India*.
Find Ashneer online on:
TWITTER @Ashneer_Grover
LINKEDIN @in/Ashneer
INSTAGRAM @ashneer.grover

DOGLAPAN

THE **HARD TRUTH** ABOUT **LIFE** AND **START-UPS**

ASHNEER GROVER

BUSINESS

An imprint of Penguin Random House

PENGUIN BUSINESS

USA | Canada | UK | Ireland | Australia
New Zealand | India | South Africa | China

Penguin Business is part of the Penguin Random House group of companies
whose addresses can be found at global.penguinrandomhouse.com

Published by Penguin Random House India Pvt. Ltd
4th Floor, Capital Tower 1, MG Road,
Gurugram 122 002, Haryana, India

First published in Penguin Business by Penguin Random House India 2022

10 9 8 7 6 5 4 3 2 1

ISBN 9780143460695

Typeset in Adobe Garamond Pro by Manipal Technologies Limited, Manipal

www.penguin.co.in

This book is dedicated to my wife, Madhuri Jain Grover,
my parents, Neeru and Ashok Grover,
and my kids, Avyukt and Mannat.
Thanks for making me whoever I am today!

Contents

Contents

Prologue

25 January 2022, 4 p.m.

'Joining back on 1st Feb'. That was the subject line of the email I had shot off to the board of directors that cold January evening. Earlier that month, I had been coerced into going on a voluntary leave of absence from BharatPe, a company worth US$3 billion (over Rs 20,000 crore) that I had built painstakingly at an unprecedented pace over the last three and a half years as its founder and managing director.

The whole of January had been a blur—I was hit relentlessly by one controversy after another. What started with a ransom call became a leaked audio, and then became leaked legal notices and arbitrary statements by Kotak bank. While the nation was enjoying *Shark Tank India* and celebrating the new wave of entrepreneurship that was taking the country and millions of TV screens by storm every weeknight from 9–10 p.m., I was personally fighting a bloody board battle aimed at wresting control of BharatPe from me. During the last week of the month I was preoccupied handling deceit, betrayal and politics by my own co-founder, hired management and thankless investors at BharatPe.

Once I proceeded on the so-called voluntary leave, I found out that the locks at BharatPe's Malviya Nagar office had been changed, the CCTV cameras had been switched off, my office and desktop had been broken into and bouncers had been stationed there. Not only were the events absolutely bizarre, but my writing to the board seeking an explanation for this gross overreach was met with absolute silence. Clearly, I had a lot to deal with. But for the time being, I was relieved that the issue with Kotak hadn't been escalated further and that the bigoted press had lost interest in it. It was time for me to resume office and focus on the next phase of growth for the business, or so I thought as I sent out that intimation of rejoining office.

25 January 2022, 4.52 p.m.

Sitting at my desk at home, with the light January sun falling over my shoulders, I was thinking through the many problems I needed to solve, especially as we had to operationalize the newly acquired banking licence at Unity SFB, the first-ever licence granted by the Reserve Bank of India (RBI) to an Indian fintech company, and complete the impending takeover of the beleaguered Punjab and Maharashtra Cooperative (PMC) Bank. That it wasn't VSS, or Sachin Bansal, but Ashneer Grover who had won the first and only bank licence given to a fintech was no mean achievement—one that, I was certain, would take the company to even greater heights. But it was also a great responsibility, as we had to first give 10 lakh depositors access to their capital, which had been stuck in their PMC bank accounts for almost two years.

My thought process was broken with the ping of an email hitting my inbox. 'Shorter Notice for 11th Board Meeting', its subject line read. To my surprise, within less than an hour of my

informing the board that I planned to resume office, I was sent
a mail from the company secretary at BharatPe, informing me
of a board meeting being called at short notice, within the next
three hours. We were to meet at 8 p.m. the same day on Zoom.
A bigger shock awaited me when I clicked on the file marked
'Agenda'. Item number 5 stared at me; it said, 'To consider &
accept the recommendation of the review committee to require
Mr. Ashneer Grover to be on leave till March 31, 2022.'

25 January 2022, 8 p.m.

'My name is Ashneer Grover. I am attending this meeting
on Zoom from New Delhi. There is no one else in the room
with me.'

The mandatory roll call, in hindsight, was perhaps the only
predictable part of this meeting. The chairman, Rajnish Kumar,
joined ten minutes late, and his first order of business was to ask
the Shardul Amarchand Mangaldas (Shardul Amarchand) and
Alvarez & Marsal team to leave the virtual meeting. Why had
they been invited in the first place to a board meeting if they were
supposed to leave? Wasn't the chairman privy to the list of invitees
to the meeting?

As the meeting began, it was stated that a resolution had
been passed to set up a two-member committee to assess the
corporate governance practices of the company. This committee,
constituted on 22 January 2022, had engaged the services of the
law firm Shardul Amarchand Mangaldas & Co. on 23 January.
In turn, they had engaged the services of the accounting firm
Alvarez & Marsal. In fact, the engagement of Alvarez & Marsal
was being brought up before the board for the very first time on
25 January.

To my utter shock, I was further being told that Alvarez
& Marsal had already come up with some alleged preliminary

findings. What's more, on the basis of these findings, none of which I was privy to, the board's proposal was to put me on a compulsory leave of absence and strip me of my powers as MD.

Some days later, I would go on to learn from media reports (no less) that the interim report of Alvarez & Marsal was dated as early as 24 January 2022. In which case, I was to believe that they had issued the report within one day of appointment and even before their official engagement by the board. In my entire career, I had never seen an instance of a lawyer or an accounting firm being appointed in a day—*yahaan toh inhone kaam bhi khatm kar diya ek din mein*; they'd even released a report in a day.

Even in my stunned state—as I felt severely let down, with a blatant conspiracy brewing against me—I asked for an opportunity to present my views before agenda item number 5 would be taken up by the board and I would be asked to drop off. I raised objections about the need for and composition of the review committee, and said that it did not comply with the shareholders' agreement and the articles of association of the company. I also pointed out that the corporate governance review covered the entire company and not only me; so by that logic, everyone should be on leave. If I was being singled out, was there any complaint against me? At whose behest was the law firm appointed?

My questions were met with deafening silence at the other end. Then I heard the chairman, Rajnish Kumar, saying, 'You may drop off from the call now, as we need to put the proposal to vote.' I would find out later that the proposal was passed unanimously, of course.

All of this, interestingly, when I did not have any communication from the board accusing me of any wrongdoing and when the so-called review was meant to be a review of 'corporate governance policies, practices & codes of the Company'.

26 January 2022

Yet another email—an outcome of the 25 January meeting!

This time, I was instructed to go on compulsory leave till 31 March 2022 and not to come to office or interact with the press, employees or shareholders, business partners, customers, vendors or any other person associated with the company, pending the governance report. For good measure, I was also instructed to return my laptop.

Just like that, from being celebrated as the most successful new-age founder of a unicorn, one who believed in speaking his mind, one who got start-ups and entrepreneurship into mainstream conversation through *Shark Tank India*, one who had earned millions of dollars for his investors and employees, I had been rendered persona non grata. While the building of the company had taken over forty-two painstaking months, the ouster was done in a matter of hours, in a pre-planned move.

The press—or rather, the tabloids operating in India in the garb of business news outlets—was once again having a field day, operating with no qualms or integrity, publishing 'news' fed to them for rewards. 'BharatPe likely to fire co-founder Ashneer Grover amid fraud concerns,' reported a leading business daily as early as 30 January, quoting 'undisclosed people familiar with the development'.

If this were an episode from *Shark Tank India*, I would probably have been tempted to say, '*Ye sab doglapan hai,*' a phrase that captured the imagination of young, emphatic India. Now, maybe I should just say, '*Picture abhi baaki hai, mere dost.*'

1

Malviya Nagar: Where It All Began

'*Ladka toh refugee hai.*'

I couldn't believe my ears. After all I, a Delhi-born boy to Delhi-born parents, was being referred to as a refugee formally, for the first time in my adult life; that too, by none other than my would-be in-laws. This was in 2003, a full fifty-six years after my grandparents had landed in Delhi, from Multan district in Pakistan, after Partition. No marks for guessing that it was meant not as a statement of fact but as a reminder of *aukaat* for a service-class Punjabi who had won the heart of their most beloved Baniya 'Jain' daughter, who came from a business family. It's another matter that this rather persistent refugee went on to attend the most premier educational institutes, landed a plum job and eventually won the family's heart and their daughter's hand.

The original refugees in question, namely my paternal grandparents, were allotted a 200-guz plot in Malviya Nagar, a refugee colony, when they landed in Delhi with their siblings and children in tow. It was on this plot that six independent floors, of 100 guz each, were built. Out of these, house number 90/20, popularly known as 'Nabbe Bees', was to later become my home address for the longest time.

As a child, I remember pestering my grandmother to tell me stories of their lives back in Multan. I loved to see the twinkle in her eye as she reminisced about the past and spoke at length about their fields or *khet*, as she referred to them. The one story that she would always tell me was about how, if the entire khet had to be covered on foot, one would need to leave early in the morning, and even then one would only be back the next day. In turn, I would egg her on with, '*Haan haan, aap toh fasal bote hue jaate the aur kat-te hue aate the* (Of course, you would sow the seeds on your way up and harvest the produce on your way back).' Growing up, the story stayed with me as a great reminder of the fact that even when that 200-guz house replaced the large expanse of their fields, it did little to dampen their spirits. In fact, they never recounted the horror of Partition—just fond memories of the past life.

The Tale of the Pandavas

Any account of the life of my grandparents wouldn't be complete without this rather curious story. Legend has it that a Peer baba read my grandmother's face and made a prophecy. '*Tumhare yahaan paanch Paandav paida honge* (You will be blessed with five sons),' he had said. With the birth of her first son, the prophesy seemed to be coming true. So my uncle was named Yudhisthira, after the eldest of the Pandavas. Only their next child happened to be a girl, leading everyone to dismiss the Peer baba's prophecy as hogwash. But they were proved wrong, as my grandparents did go on to have five sons, and two daughters. And no, the other sons weren't named after the rest of the Pandavas; so we didn't have the star cast of the Mahabharata at home.

Even though in the hierarchy of the five sons, my dad was at a distant number four, my grandparents lived with us, while my dad's four brothers and their families stayed on different independent floors. Back then, much as I loved my grandparents, I must admit that there were days when I thought my cousins had it much better. After all, they didn't have to play the default host for every function simply because the eldest Grovers, namely my grandparents, lived there. Where our house was like a mela, with a sea of relatives thronging it, their houses offered much more privacy.

In hindsight, this appears to be such juvenile thinking, especially as I realize the kind of blessings I have received. In fact, I feel a lot of that karma came through, as among our extended family I ended up studying the most and, as it turned out, achieving the most in my career. The only time my grandparents moved away briefly to live in another unit in the 200-guz plot was when I was in high school, and they thought I could do with some more space. But the act resulted in so much emotional pain to us as a family that my dad decided to buy a 200-square-yard builder floor right opposite where we lived. While the house cost us a whopping Rs 32 lakh in 2002—a huge amount in those days—the sense of fulfilment of living with my grandparents under the same roof once again was priceless.

My grandfather, Shri Nand Lal Grover, was an extremely well-respected figure in the community, especially as he set up the Arya Samaj of Malviya Nagar as well as the accompanying primary school. Ours was a liberal family; growing up, I didn't see my grandparents or parents take to any elaborate religious rituals or idol worship. We never went to the mandir except on Janmashtami, to see the *jhaankis*. Instead, what we had—and these were part of my early years—were frequent havans in the Arya Samaj tradition that were meant as acts of purification and acknowledging nature as the real god. I grew up an atheist mostly.

Curiously, when I went on to set up BharatPe, its leased office had its boundary wall touching the same Arya Samaj, something that I recognized as less of a coincidence and more of a blessing even at that time. I ensured that the inauguration of this office, and of every subsequent BharatPe office, was marked by a havan, something that was absolutely ingrained within me. When BharatPe turned into a unicorn—and for the longest time it was the only unicorn with a Delhi PIN code—I knew it was due to the blessings of my grandparents.

The board that said 'Grover, Lalla & Mehta'—outside the chartered accountancy firm that my dad ran—was another familiar sign for me, growing up. Many years later, even when he had bought the firm, he continued to run it with the names of his original partners, in recognition of their connection. I had an early association with my dad's firm—not as a bookkeeper but as a water-soaker. Come monsoon, and his basement office in Malviya Nagar would be flooded. Some of us kids would then be called upon to draw out the water with pumps. The sense of importance that we would feel on being entrusted with such a critical job and the fun that we had in the process were both incomparable.

By the time I was in fifth grade, my mom had joined a school as a teacher. If there was one thing that she wanted to give her children, it was good education and a lot of exposure. Her dad, my nanaji, was a banker and worked at the erstwhile Imperial Bank, which was rechristened the State Bank of India after the Government of India and the Reserve Bank of India assumed its joint ownership in 1955. While he had been posted all over the country, he retired as the GM, Loan Disbursals, from SBI's Mumbai office, one that I frequented as a child. It was fascinating to see his imposing office at Nariman Point. The tall SBI building, with the amazing view of the sea in the background, and the imposing Mumbai skyline had me in awe of a banker's life.

Amin Chand Pyare Lal Jalandhar Wale

That was the origin of the name of my school, although the name had been shortened to the more fancy-sounding Apeejay. While it may have lost some ground today to the many international schools that have since made their appearance, it was considered to be a decent school in those days, and I have extremely fond memories of that time. The school was located in Sheikh Sarai in Delhi. One day, my grandfather went and spoke to the principal, one Mr Chaudhary, and I got enrolled in the school. Each day it was a ritual for my grandfather to walk me to school through the neighbouring Khidki Gaon and for us to make a pitstop in the fields to pluck mooli and munch on it on the way to school.

Interestingly, the kids in my school fell into four groups based on their standing in life. There was a 'Bong' group, largely comprising residents of CR Park, the capital's Bengali hub; then there were the rich kids from tony Greater Kailash or what is fashionably called GK; the cool kids from the Sheikh Sarai self-financing-scheme flats, which were akin to the original condos; followed by the lesser kids from the adjoining Malviya Nagar, such as yours truly. If there was one person who could be credited with briefly uniting these groups, it had to be—surprise of all surprises—the Bollywood actress Tisca Chopra.

Tisca (Arora) Chopra was the daughter of our then principal, Mr Arora, and her movie *Platform*, in which she co-starred with Ajay Devgn, had released when we were in school. Conversations about how gorgeous she was (and how starstruck we were) resonated in the school canteen in those days. Every boy in school secretly imagined replacing the intense-eyed Mr Devgn and romancing Ms Chopra on the silver screen. Our connection to her, no matter how far-fetched, added a dash of glamour to our otherwise mundane lives. Incidentally, there have been many TV personalities who graduated from our school—Manish Paul,

Ridhi Dogra and Nidhi Razdan, to name a few. Many years later, and unexpectedly on TV, also me.

A defining point in my life during my schooldays has to be a trip that I took with my mom, sister and my nanaji to meet my uncle (mama) who lived in Canada. This was much before the time when travelling abroad had become fashionable and flooding your social media posts with pictures from exotic countries, even more so. To say that I was charmed by the life I saw would be an understatement. Not only did I spend time in Canada, we also travelled to the US and the UK before heading back home. That one trip opened my eyes to a world of possibilities. I realized that the life we were living and the life we could potentially live were very different.

While I was an average student up until fifth grade, by sixth grade I had developed a drive to study. Not only was I diligent about completing my work, but I was also quite competitive and absolutely hated losing marks. If there was someone who faced collateral damage because of this, it had to be my sister. Four years my junior, Aashima was good in her studies, but I had placed the bar rather high for her. '*Oh, ye Ashneer ki behen hai* (Oh, she is Ashneer's sister)!' was the typical response my mom received when she went to her class after hearing glowing praises from my teachers during the PTMs. Naturally, the four years that my sister spent in school after I graduated turned out to be the most enjoyable for her.

Heartbreak

It was during the last two years of my school life that I made my first and only girlfriend. '*Bhai ab cool dude ban gaya hai* (Our friend is a cool dude now)' was the reaction I would get from my gang of friends as I entered the couples club. But the euphoria was short-lived, as one fine day the girl declared that I was becoming too possessive about her and drifted away. After having suitably mourned my re-entry into singledom, I thankfully decided that it was time to focus on building a career.

While my dad ran his own CA practice, I was clear that it was not something I wanted to pursue. I realized early on that a CA practice, or that of a doctor or lawyer, had very little scalability and that success there was totally based on the number of hours you put in. Besides, I had travelled with my dad extensively while he was conducting audits at the NTPC plant in Orissa and had discovered that the real joy of creation lay in engineering and not in bookkeeping. This was a sentiment that my father shared with me, as he would rather see me creating value as opposed to managing somebody else's books.

Irrespective of the career I chose, one thing that my family background had made clear to me was that I had to rise in life by dint of my ability. In fact, the interesting thing about our refugee colony was that it was a great leveller. Each one of us literally began from ground zero, or should I say with a 200-guz plot. What we built from thereon was totally up to us. I, for one, was determined to make it big; a subconscious part of me perhaps wanted to make good, despite the setback that my family had faced during Partition.

2

'Teri Hawa Kitni Hai?'

That was the first question I got asked as I entered the hallowed portals of IIT Delhi. Having made up my mind to pursue engineering, I was finally at the mecca for all aspiring engineers. For all my academic rigour and a fairly decent rank at JEE, my mind drew a complete blank at this question I was asked. For the life of me, I couldn't understand how I was expected to quantify how much air (*hawa*) belonged to me. To make matters worse, I was staring at rather scary faces. The big beards and that intimidating look in the eyes of those 'seniors' were enough to have anyone reconsider their IIT dream.

The seniors had only one agenda—to do unto others as had been done unto them—namely, to rag the juniors. Until perhaps they took pity on my plight and reframed the question as: What was your All India Rank? (AIR, or hawa, as they called it!) I had been told all along that once you cleared JEE, life was 'set'. But here, on day one itself, people were hell-bent on making my IIT dream into a nightmare!

To make it to this dream destination, of course, involved a lot of rigorous work and sacrifices. I had joined FIITJEE classes that were known to churn out a number of IITians and had spent two extremely hectic years there. Each day after school, I would barely finish my lunch when my mom would already be calling out to me to rush, as she would drop me to the coaching centre. On the way back, I would jostle to catch the infamous DTC bus route number 503, which would drop me home to Malviya Nagar.

Besides the many hacks that FIITJEE taught me in order to crack the coveted Joint Entrance Examination, what I also witnessed there at first hand was the innate strength of a branch of a guava tree or *amrood ki tehni*, as it was popularly referred to. That was a pivotal tool that the maths teacher used with all his might, to drive home some important lessons. He would refer to us as *bhutte ke khet waale bandar* (cornfield monkeys)! Legend has it that monkeys would often raid cornfields in villages. The first time the monkey would pull out a corn, he would keep it under his armpit. Then he would pull out yet another corn and do the same, dropping the first corn in the process. At the end of the raid, you would have a devastated cornfield while the monkey would still be going back with only one corn. That, to the maths teacher, was representative of how we studied, conveniently sieving out of memory the previously learnt lesson each time a new lesson was taught and becoming the proverbial 'bhutte ke khet waale bandar' in the process.

It was no monkey business, though, to manage to climb my way up to the second batch of the FIITJEE group, each jump indicative of the probability of getting a good rank at the Joint Entrance Examination. Come the actual entrance exam, and it was quite another story, as I thought I had blown my chance with the very first paper. No marks for guessing that the paper under question was mathematics! I remember sitting in the car post the exam and literally weeping while telling my parents that there wasn't a chance that I would make it and that I shouldn't even waste my time attending the remaining exams. It so happened that there was another car in the parking lot, whose passenger was also shedding copious tears at her plight. The two sets of parents immediately convinced their wards that the maths misery was widespread. As they say, misery loves company. Based on my understanding of this collective suffering, I went on to attempt the other papers. Thankfully so, as the results revealed that my All India Rank was 1823!

When the result was declared, the atmosphere at home was euphoric, to say the least. I was the only child from my school that year to make it. Importantly, our entire refugee colony had got together at our home that evening, every heart beating with pride at the thought that one of their own was now ready to take on the new world order!

The bubble burst quickly when I realized that while my rank, 1823, could lead me to an IIT, there wasn't a chance of my making it to the much-coveted computer science course. Ours was the millennium batch that had big dreams to study computers and make it to the US of A. To my disappointment, I realized that the best I could hope to get was chemical engineering at IIT Guwahati. If at all I wanted to make it to IIT Delhi, I would have to settle for either civil or textile engineering. My dad had done a lot of audit work with IIT Delhi and knew a couple of professors there. He put me on to one of them, who advised me that making an entry into IIT Delhi would open doorways to my future and that I should think beyond the choice of the course. It was on this advice that I tore up my already-filled form and stated in the new one IIT Delhi, civil engineering, as my first choice—which I went on to pursue.

Of Bus Routes and Traffic Lights

To be honest, though, apart from this professor's advice, what also led me to IIT Delhi was, believe it or not, the lack of traffic lights between my home at Malviya Nagar and the IIT Delhi campus. It so happened that while I had mentioned civil engineering at IIT Delhi as my preferred choice, pulled by the appeal of the electronics course, I decided to go for the orientation at Delhi College of Engineering (DCE), another coveted institute that I had made it to.

A dear friend, Shubhang Shankar, who had also set his eyes on IIT but got convinced to explore the course at DCE, accompanied me. Truth be told, once you have witnessed the imposing IIT campus, no other campus even comes close. Nonetheless, we made our way to attend the orientation at DCE. While we were being told the many nuances of the courses, Shankar had an urgent question to ask the panel at DCE. While several pairs of serious-looking eyes turned to him expecting that his question would lead them to further enlightenment, his question filled that tense DCE hall with nervous giggles.

'Which bus route would I need to take to get to DCE?' went his earnest query. While many thought he was asking an inane question and even being disrespectful, for him the question was anything but that. It was actually his question that led to a shift within me and made me realize that there was a lot of merit in the fact that I lived next door to IIT Delhi, and lo and behold—there also wasn't a single traffic light between my house at Malviya Nagar and the institute. That helped me make the decision, one that I have never regretted!

It was actually this proximity to home that later enabled my IIT journey as a day scholar as opposed to being a hosteller, which, among other things, saved me from some rather gruesome ragging episodes that many of my batchmates were subjected to. In fact, a very good friend of mine from FIITJEE, Ashutosh Mathur, had made it to the chemical engineering programme and was a hosteller. At one point, he was ready to go back home on account of the ragging that was really awful. At alumni meets even today, the common refrain of all hostellers is, '*Bahot phat ti thi*,' referring to the ragging they were subjected to.

The Two-Hour Rank-Holder

When you are being pushed to give IIT preparations your best shot, the general idea is that once you have cracked JEE, you don't have to worry too much about your future. Nothing could be further from the truth. Having been fed liberally on this advice, I, of course, decided to take life a little easy. With the net result that I landed up with an SGPA of 7.3 in the first semester! Shankar (the guy who had wanted to understand bus routes at the DCE orientation) knew better and managed an SGPA of above 9. The fact that his stream changed on account of that from civil to mechanical came as a big blow to me. So much so that I like to think this event paved the way for my future at IIT. That, and the fact that I was counselled by another day scholar and a dear friend, Parakram Khandpur, who was in the sought-after computer science course, with an AIR of 33; he told me that without hard work, the IIT dream would remain just that—a pipe dream!

I had decided that it was time to get back to my hard-working avatar. From the 7.3 SGPA of the first semester, I quickly hit a 9 in the second semester and thereafter never stopped short of 9.5, semester after semester. In fact, in the last semester I even hit a perfect 10—that revered 'dassi'. A 'dassi' in the last semester is actually a rare event, since by then people have either got through campus placements or have their eyes set on joining a master's programme, and there is no incentive for getting this high a grade. For me, though, it was about outdoing myself and proving a point. While I was departmental rank 2 right from the second semester, when I had consciously decided to turn my fortunes around, with this perfect score in the last semester I graduated to department rank 1 . . . but only for a period of two hours!

It so happened that while the final grades were published and put up on the notice board, the erstwhile departmental rank 1 went crying to the prof. saying, '*Meri zindagi kharab ho gayi* (My life is ruined).' While he had worked consistently all along, he had lost out in the final semester. The prof. decided to reward his consistency and grant him an additional grade that once again turned him into department rank 1. It was a big blow for me, as I missed out on the accolades and the medal that would come to the first rank-holder, despite being one.

This incident has stayed in my mind as a big marker, as I see this theme recurring in several aspects of my life. I have been a late bloomer for sure. Well, but perhaps good things come to those who wait!

A Rejected Visa and Redemption

'Your visa application has been rejected.' The hurt that this one sentence generated still rankles. I was a tenth-grader at the time and had applied for a Canadian visa to visit my mama during the summer vacation by myself. Even though the rejection was on technical grounds, of not having attached an NOC from my school, it hurt. So much so that while I have travelled to more than fifty countries since, that 'rejected' visa application still hounds me.

When IIT presented a chance to redeem this visa rejection by way of an exchange programme, I jumped at the offer. To my delight, I cracked the interview that qualified me for this programme in France, along with five other batchmates. The Institut National des Sciences Appliquées de Lyon, or INSA Lyon, as it was popularly referred to, was to be my home for the next year. Both the institute as well as the exchange programme were much sought-after. The cherry on the cake was the fact that you didn't have to pay through your nose. While you paid your regular fees at IIT, the French student involved in the exchange would pay his fees in France without being hit by the exchange rate.

I was in luck for one other reason—I had figured out that a scholarship of as much as 600 euros a month, which was available for students pursuing their master's in France, was, that year, open to students pursuing their bachelor's course as well. The dilemma that I faced was that only two scholarships were being given out, and if I were to share this information with my other batchmates, my odds of getting the scholarship would become 1/6. While the student holding department rank 1 knew of this change, the two of us went on to apply for the scholarship and received it. It is another matter that when we landed in France and had to report for the processing of our scholarship, it was mighty awkward to face the other four people who were glaring at us for our not having told them of the opportunity.

Set at the confluence of the Rhône and Saône rivers, Lyon is the third-largest city in France, after Paris and Marseille, and is a lovely place to be in. The year that I spent in Europe has to count among the high points in my life. We reached Lyon nearly one and a half months before our classes were to begin, and we used that time to learn French and, of course, to explore Europe on a shoestring.

That year spent in France exposed me to an exceptional educational system. In the early days I was spellbound at the sight of French students attending classes with pencil boxes that had pens of different colours. Their meticulousness could be seen in the fact that they wrote what the prof. was saying in class in one colour, took down what was written on the board in another colour and followed that up with their thoughts about the subject in yet another colour. Even when I came back to India, that rigour stayed with me. Importantly, I realized that while the Indian education system took pride in its toppers, the French system took pride in the bottom of their batch. They celebrated the fact that even the lowest in the marks hierarchy understood the basic concepts.

Besides spending an academically enriching year, I made the most of the year by travelling the whole of Europe and even doing a solo trip to the UK. For all the IIT smarts and those great SGPAs, we also ended up doing a number of stupid things. In Italy, with a batchmate, I drove a Vespa, relishing the fact that there were no traffic lights, only to realize that we had driven through at least twenty red lights that hung from cables, while we were looking for poles. In Switzerland, we casually sauntered into a railway tunnel in Interlaken until we felt some tremors and miraculously jumped off to the side just in time to see a train whoosh past!

I also made some lasting friendships in France as a part of the Lyon international programme, where you were hosted by a local family. Not only did I visit them nearly every week, so strong was our connection that when I was to travel back to India, the gentleman drove me down from Lyon to the Geneva airport almost one and a half hours away. No marks for guessing that I had chosen Geneva as my boarding destination because the flight from Geneva was far cheaper! Importantly, courtesy of the scholarship that I had won, when I got back to India I had saved enough money, so that I didn't have to ask my parents for any money for my further education. As a matter of fact, I've been financially independent since 2002.

The one thing that the year spent in France did for me was to take away my rose-tinted glasses through which one looked at foreign locations as the panacea for all troubles. For all the fun that I had in France, I also experienced the loneliness that staying abroad brings in its wake. Particularly in the last two months, when I pursued my internship in Lyon while my batchmates had moved to other cities, I experienced a kind of isolation that was very draining. Back in India, I was clear that I no longer wanted to go to Stanford or MIT for my master's, as that would mean building a career overseas. On the contrary, I was sure that the discipline and rigour that I had come armed with had to be put to use to bell the cat (read: crack the CAT exam).

3

Mads: The Love of My Life

If my choice of joining the coaching institute Career Launcher, for cracking the CAT exam, was strategic, choosing its centre was even more so. Ditching the one that was opposite IIT in SDA Market in Delhi, I decided to opt for the slightly distant Kailash Colony centre, on account of a very important fact: the girls there were more happening! And I knew very well that this was the last chance for me to find a girl before I got into the rigours of an MBA course and a job thereafter. I have to say that the place lived up to my expectations, as this was where I met the love of my life: my wife, Madhuri.

Turns out that destiny had a big role to play in getting us together. I was actually supposed to be in a batch that began fifteen minutes earlier than the batch I'd started to attend, erroneously. This was where I first saw one of the most fashionable people I have ever met. My earliest memory of the class at Career Launcher—which was meant to prepare us to study management—concerns the fashion management of this girl who had come wearing a top with multicoloured stripes that was coordinated with a similar hairband and socks; she also carried a diary with—you guessed it—the same multicoloured stripes. To say that I was blown away would be an understatement. While I was super confident about cracking the CAT exam, I knew that it would require much greater effort to win her over. All I knew about her at the time was her name, Madhuri Jain, and the fact that she was a NIFT graduate. With just that limited information, in true Bollywood style, I proclaimed to my friend Ashutosh Mathur that one day I would marry this girl.

An Unflattering Feedback

While Madhuri was extremely reserved, I didn't let go of any opportunity to speak with her. In fact, I pestered her for a lunch date at the 'cool' hangout place of the time: The Big Chill Café in East of Kailash! Because of my perseverance, Madhuri decided to first seek feedback on me from her NIFT colleague Ankita, who had studied with me at Apeejay School. She asked Ankita if she knew a guy named 'Ash-noor'. Well, her feedback has to go down in history as the most unflattering feedback on me: '*Ash-noor nahi Ashneer. Wo na ainvayi hai, usse door hi rahiyo* (He is quite unremarkable, stay away from him.' These were her exact words. To my credit, despite this, I managed to convince Madhuri to come for lunch, which turned out to be the beginning of the many dates we went on subsequently.

From the family perspective, though, the two of us were as different as chalk and cheese. I come from a non-veg-eating Punjabi family, she from a family of pure vegetarian Baniya Jains. I am from a service-class background, hers is a well-established business family. I lived in a 200-guz flat, her family had a large bungalow. I have one sibling, she has five. I came from the metropolis Delhi, she is from Panipat. But none of this mattered, as I was head over heels in love with her.

My first port of call, when it came to introducing Madhuri to my family, was my nani, my maternal grandmother. A big proponent of looking at every life situation through a positive lens, she finds her strength from attending satsangs and has even overcome a battle with cancer with her characteristic positivity. Once I had gained her implicit approval, it was time for a bigger task: to have my mom meet Madhuri. A typical Punju mother, she never shied away from making her criteria for her would-be daughter-in-law known. 'The girl should be good-looking.' This meant fair and, therefore, lovely. Well, Madhuri met those standards for sure. I remember my mom looking at Madhuri from top to toe and later offering me two pieces of feedback. The first was that she didn't look like a Baniya (essentially too fair for her expectation of Baniyas); second, that although she wasn't too tall, she had the confidence of carrying herself in flat footwear. That did it at my end.

When it came to convincing Madhuri's side of the family, though, it was quite another ball game. For one, we had a bad start. Madhuri's dad had given her a Mitsubishi Lancer along with a driver, to navigate her way in Delhi, while the family was stationed in Panipat. When we started dating, we would often go around the city in her car. Drivers are known to cause havoc, and hers lived up to this reputation. He took it as his moral responsibility to inform her parents that their daughter was seeing someone. All hell broke loose in Madhuri's family. On hearing the driver's narrative, her dad thought that his eldest progeny had let him down and misused the freedom that she had been given. When he had a little more information about the boy in question, his grouse was further strengthened. The fact that I was a Punju who was still to land a half-decent job was a big red flag for her family, especially for her dad and her maternal uncle. Before I knew it, Madhuri's dad had summoned her back to Panipat.

It was amid this high drama rocking my personal life that I went on to give my CAT exam. The CAT exam that year was referred to as the 'leaky CAT', as the paper had allegedly been leaked. In fact, we were informed that we had to sit for the exam all over again, right after coming out of the examination hall. When the centre for the second exam was announced—it turned out to be the same centre where I had appeared for my JEE—I instantly knew that there was some cosmic connection and that I would get through. And get through I did! I was nothing short of euphoric to know that on paper I now had the best academic combination—IIT Delhi and IIM Ahmedabad. Importantly, I thought maybe this could change my standing in the eyes of Madhuri's family. I was hoping that the reputation of the institute would rub off on Madhuri's dad and that he would see me in a cooler light. But it wasn't to be as I realized that for Baniyas how much you earn is far more important than your degrees! He was, at best, noncommittal. Being the family-oriented person that Madhuri is, she was certain that if anything had to work out, it had to be with the blessings of her parents.

Madhuri, Alias Ankit Khanna

The one thing that my moving to Ahmedabad did was that Madhuri was allowed to come back to Delhi from Panipat and live in a PG. By now she had started to work for the designer Satya Paul. All my visits to Delhi from Ahmedabad now supposedly had a pitstop at my IIT Delhi friend Ankit Khanna's house (read Madhuri's PG) for a day, before I headed home to meet my parents. Of course, Madhuri had to be super careful to let me into the PG. The fact that the owner of Madhuri's PG lived in the same building, albeit on another floor, meant that I had to wait till their lights were switched off. For two full years, such was the level of adventure we had to be able to meet each other.

Life at IIMA

In the meantime, settling in at IIM wasn't particularly easy. Technically, it was the first time that I was living away from home, unless I counted the year I had spent in France while at IIT. As if the rigours of IIM by themselves weren't enough, in the first few days we also had our seniors play a hoax on us. The period was marked with instructions such as: if you aren't up until 3 a.m. every morning, you aren't cut out to be at IIM. So much was the psychological pressure of fitting in that we had instances of people sleeping with their lights on, to make the others believe that they were studying until the wee hours of the morning. I found it all extremely untenable. Even when I was finally told that this was a hoax being played on us, it did little to improve my perception of IIM.

Overall, whereas I had found people at IIT to be naturally super sharp, the folks at IIM seemed more driven! Importantly, while at IIT people were exploring their potential, at IIM they were driven by the singular objective of landing a plum 'Day Zero' job. Clearly, IIM was a zero-sum game and more a placement school than anything else. We were living like crabs, waiting to pull the other down to be able to move up ourselves, something that I detested. That explained why, while I had several batchmates at IIM, there were very few genuine friendships. In fact, most of my friends at IIM were those who had made the journey with me from IIT.

If you had to succeed at IIM, the one skill that you needed the most was networking, a skill that I didn't quite pride myself on. In fact, I was a socially awkward person and would interact only with people I knew well; put me in a room full of strangers, and I would clam up. At some level, it's the Gemini in me that makes me a bit of a split personality. The long and short of the networking story is that while many of my batchmates successfully networked for the prestigious Goldman Sachs summer internship in New York or Tokyo, I had to make do with summer placements at KPMG, despite my academic grades—which didn't go down very well with me.

Come the second year, and things finally started to get better. This was largely because the final placements were dependent only on the first-year grades. There was, therefore, that much less reason for people to pull each other down. I began to notice far friendlier and more relaxed versions of the very same people who were out to get you in the first year. In fact, this was the one time that I also stepped out of my comfort zone to explore things I never thought I would do. I became a part of the exchange committee at IIM and even participated in a play, where I essayed the role of the eunuch *sakhi* of a maharani, something that wasn't quite up my alley.

Another interesting event that I remember from those times is the visit of Vijay Mallya, the beer baron, to our campus. Sauntering into the auditorium wearing a beige coat and red sunglasses, he seemed to be playing to the gallery and received a standing ovation. When he spoke, he left an impact on us on account of his candidness. Sharing his life story, he reminisced about how he had lost his dad when he was twenty-five and how that suddenly pushed him into full media glare. Asking us whether a twenty-five-year-old would be more inclined towards parties or satsangs, he explained how the media had built his playboy image only because he was seen frequenting some parties and it suited their narrative. The larger point he made was that in India, our natural view of a well-to-do businessman is that he must have used unfair means to amass his riches, and, therefore, we are reluctant to celebrate success stories in India. Even though the subsequent turn of events in Mallya's own life didn't stand up to this theory, the lesson still holds.

Day Zero

Soon it was time for the famous 'Day Zero'—a creative mathematical nomenclature at IIM, referring to the day when big recruiters visit the campus.

This was the day we had firms such as Lehman Brothers, Barclay's, Goldman Sachs, McKinsey and the like making an appearance. But for me, Day Zero turned out to be quite anticlimactic, as, to my immense embarrassment, I couldn't crack a single job. My way of coping with this huge setback was to switch off my phone, hit the bed and sleep. Until I was literally shaken up by my batchmates, who informed me that Barclay's wanted to have another interview round with me. Having shortlisted candidates at IIM Ahmedabad, they had proceeded to IIM Calcutta with a view to selecting some students from there. Having found a difference in quality, they were now keen to enlist some more students from Ahmedabad. If anything, this only prolonged the misery for me, as I didn't make it through the second round either.

What I did have subsequently, on Day One, was a good interview with Kotak Bank. In fact, the interviewer was an IIM Ahmedabad graduate himself, and I marvelled at him for asking some technical, finance-related questions as opposed to the stereotypical 'Where do you see yourself five years from now', the answer to which is generally as meaningless to the interviewer as it is to the interviewee. My stint at IIM had made me realize that finance *muhje chamakta tha*, I quite loved the subject. What also excited me about the Kotak opportunity was that by now I was very certain that I didn't want a consulting role. In fact, if anything, I have an inherent hatred for consultants. *Baaton ka khate hai*, they make money from creative storytelling—a task I wasn't up to. The job at Kotak, on the other hand, would help me hone my chops at hardcore finance. What also tilted the balance in favour of Kotak was the fact that at the time it had a joint venture with Goldman Sachs. If I hadn't been able to make it to Goldman Sachs, I thought I was at the next best place. Only, ironically, I didn't know then, that by the time I would join Kotak, its JV with Goldman Sachs would have come to an end.

This analysis notwithstanding, the absolute best thing about having this job was that Madhuri's dad finally saw some value in me and agreed to meet my parents.

A Monsoon Wedding

In the interim years while I was at IIM, Madhuri's family had been receiving a lot of *rishtas*, and great ones at that, from rich, loaded Baniya households. Somewhere, however, her dad had come to believe that if Madhuri had chosen someone for herself, perhaps it was for the best. With my having landed a good job, my stakes improved further. My offer from Kotak was for an annual CTC of Rs 8 lakh, with a Rs 3 lakh assured bonus. The way that the job was sold to us, however, was that there was a possibility of making 150–200 per cent bonus, thereby pegging the total annual earning potential at Rs 20 lakh. When I tried to sell the job to Madhuri's dad similarly, his reply was a succinct '*jitney ki lagi hai utne ki baat karo* (let's discuss what you have in hand currently)'. I realized how rooted in reality Baniya businessmen are. While we are taught to be optimistic, they have been able to make their mark while being realistic.

Well, Rs 20 lakh or not, courtesy of the job, I was officially engaged on 14 April 2006. Having agreed to the wedding, my father-in-law was in a great hurry to fix the wedding date. I joined Kotak's Mumbai office on 14 May, and I was back in Delhi in time for my monsoon wedding on 4 July. While my cousins really cursed me for having agreed to get married at the worst time of the year, I wasn't taking any chances. *Bahot papad bele the shaadi karne ke liye*, it had been one hell of a struggle to reach this place. Incidentally, Madhuri's maternal uncle didn't come around and skipped the wedding—the refugee tag couldn't be wiped off even with a decent job offer!

4

My Naukri Days

Part 1: Years at Kotak

July 2006, Mumbai

A one-BHK apartment in a slum rehabilitation society with a rent of Rs 16,000!

That was where Madhuri and I began our married life. Having moved to Mumbai by myself in May 2006, I had to quickly look for a place in time for our wedding. And this seemed like the best option, given the Rs 48,000 salary (post tax) that I drew at the time. Neel Ganga Co-op Housing Society in Lower Parel, occupied partly by the original slum dwellers and partly by new occupants, became our marital home. Even though a one-BHK in Mumbai is akin to half a drawing room in Delhi, both of us, newly married and so much in love with each other, really liked the life we were setting out to build. It seemed that the city was ready to welcome us into its fold.

The Kotak office was at Nariman Point, and it felt almost glamorous to drive through the Queen's Necklace every morning to get to work. It helped greatly that these early years marked a boomtime for investment banking. I had joined Kotak as a part of their mergers and acquisitions team, and it felt like a privilege to be a part of the institution. I had to report to a gentleman called Sughosh Moharikar, the head of M&A, who, in turn, used to report to Falguni Nayar (yes, of Nykaa fame), the overall head for investment banking. While as a new joinee, I had not, of course, met the top boss, Uday, I was in awe of him, hearing stories such as when our bosses went to him with fancy spreadsheets, all he needed to do was take out his 1980s calculator to rip the spreadsheets apart. No surprise there, as the huge reputation that he had built for himself in the investment-banking circuit spoke for itself. In fact, at one time, Kampani, Kothari and Kotak were known as the three Ks in investment banking.

Referred to as 'Lala' in the Kotak circuit, Uday was also known for his understated lifestyle. He used to own a light-blue Camry car, while his wife used to drive a Santro in those days, at a time when BMWs and Mercs were becoming common. The story goes that even though the Kotak investment banking guys were making good money, they looked poor since they couldn't spend, simply because the boss wasn't spending.

Anchor Electricals

In my first year at Kotak, I was put on a transaction where Anchor Electricals, a well-known name in the electrical accessories market, was looking for a buyer. A home-grown business, set up by two Gujarati gentlemen, Jadav Ji and Damji Bhai Shah, it had grown, from its modest roots, to be the largest electrical switch business in India. In fact, it was a great opportunity for me to have a ringside view of how Indian traditional businesses were built. For all the talk about their humble beginnings, nothing could prepare me for the moment when Atul Bhai, the elder son of one of the founders, with whom I was closely working on the sale, pointed out to a shop as we were crossing Worli Naka, to indicate that the founders used to sleep on the ground outside that shop, in the early days of setting up the business. This was a quintessential rags-to-riches story.

I had been given leeway by my boss, Vikas, to be stationed at the Anchor Electricals office, to see the deal through. For the next nine months, therefore, their office at MIDC, in Andheri, was to be my workplace along with that of my reporting manager, Neeraj. The curious part about the Anchor office was, no matter which language you spoke, the reply would always be in Gujarati. Thankfully, having spent two years in Ahmedabad, I had begun to understand the language. In fact, for the first time I realized that Gujarati was a great language to do business in, devoid of the aggression that many other languages seem to implicitly have. Even in the most heated discussions, the words or the tonality of the language did not add to the hostility.

During this period, I also travelled extensively, along with potential investors, to the Anchor plants in Kutch and Daman and Diu. While the general perception is that investment banking involves sitting in plush offices, wearing a suit and tie and staring at laptop screens, there are, in fact, many other things that you are required to do, including saving the transaction from the founder's eccentricities. I encountered several such instances. At one time, I had to ensure that Atul Bhai, who would not drink while in Mumbai but would do so when in Diu, was escorted to his room before he said anything that would spook the investors. The one incident that will always stay in my memory, though, pertains to when I was sitting in their office and there was sudden mayhem on account of a sales-tax raid. Before we knew it, the premises were sealed. 'Do you have a Kotak identity card?' I was asked by their CFO. A young associate, I nodded in the affirmative, only to be told by him to carry Rs 2 lakh in cash that was lying with him and walk out of the office.

When the sales tax officials at the gate stopped me, I flashed my Kotak ID and told them that I was here for official work. While I was allowed to go, I ended up carrying that amount in my bag for three days. For someone who had a take-home salary of Rs 48,000 in those days, this was a large amount. I was totally psyched out. My bosses saw it as a great leg-pulling opportunity and kept telling me that the sales tax officials would now knock at my door. The funny thing was that nobody from Anchor called me for the money—I had to call the CFO and ask about how and where I could hand over the money. I was finally told to 'drop it' at a store in Cuffe Parade. So ended my predicament.

The Anchor business was very fragmented since they had multiple small units. What we had to undertake was a complex transaction, whereby, in a slump sale, all the companies were sold to the parent company, in which the buying entity would finally put in the money. While there were several buyers in the fray, including Schneider Electric, Wipro and Panasonic, the deal was finally closed with Panasonic. Even though today, the Maruti and Ranbaxy deals are widely talked about, back in 2007 Anchor was the largest cross-border deal from Japan into India. While Panasonic took 80 per cent equity in the company for US$400 million, there was an earn-out built in for the balance 20 per cent for the promoters. Not only was it a great deal for Anchor, it was also big for Kotak, as our fee on the deal was as much as Rs 25 crore. 'Deal done,' I said confidently on the phone call to my boss once the fee amount had hit the Kotak account.

Having handled such a complex deal in the very first year of my career, I earned a reputation as the 'tough deal guy' in the company. On the back of that deal, I also had a great year, as I was given a 135 per cent bonus, taking my total earnings up to Rs 19 lakh that year. Clearly, I had underpromised and overdelivered on my earning expectation to my father-in-law. To celebrate, Madhuri and I decided to take a trip to the US and Canada for three weeks.

It was our much-delayed honeymoon, one that we hadn't had time for earlier. Interestingly, it has been the cheapest trip of our lives—I bought return tickets for Rs 40,000 per person as the US dollar was trading at Rs 39 in June 2007.

On our return, Madhuri got a job at Alok Industries, a textile solutions company. The fact that she could walk to her office at Peninsula Corporate Park, which was right across our building, was nothing short of luxury in a metropolis like Mumbai, where commuting takes the most part of your day. Another earning hand, of course, added to our overall comfort. Importantly, having studied at NIFT Delhi, Madhuri loved working in a related industry.

On the personal front, too, we were having a great time. While we missed our families, fortunately for us, Madhuri's elder sister lived in Mumbai. Their house at Malabar Hill was our frequent haunt. Her husband ran a business while also trading in stocks and making a lot of money in those days. Overall, we were leading a fairly glamorous South Mumbai life.

Suits and Superbikes

Luck seemed to be shining upon us at that time. In January 2008, Madhuri was headed to Heidelberg, Germany, for a work-related exhibition, before which we decided to hit a mall in Mumbai. This was the one time I wanted to splurge on myself, having earned the handsome bonus. For the first time ever, I bought an expensive suit for myself. What we were offered along with it were some raffle tickets that could win you a superbike. Never having won any lottery in my life, I promptly forgot about it, until I received a phone call one day informing me that I had won the superbike— Yamaha MT-01—worth a whopping Rs 12 lakh. I remember calling Madhuri excitedly in Germany, to share this news. After the initial euphoria waned, the practical consideration of what we would do with the bike led her to remark that we should ask the mall to give us the second prize instead: a television set. '*Baniyon wali baat mat kar*,' was my response to her, convincing her that we must collect the superbike.

It was Marc Robinson, the model and actor, who was called upon to hand over the bike. But not being sure of where I would ride the bike, I figured out some bike dealers in Mumbai and ended up selling the bike to a Parsi guy for Rs 8 lakh. I had to pay a gift tax of Rs 4 lakh and yet made a neat Rs 4 lakh, thanks to the suit which brought me an over 15x return.

* * *

As a young investment banker, I was keen on digging my teeth into various industries, and I soon got a chance to work in a new sector. The second year at Kotak saw me raise money for the real estate client Rustomjee. I spent over a year with the client, learning the nuances of the industry and eventually raising $60 million for them through SUN-Apollo, a real estate fund. So happy were the founders at Rustomjee with my efforts that post the deal, they offered me the role of CEO for their upcoming township, a prestigious Rs 1000-crore project. I was all of twenty-six at the time. I didn't take the offer, but it was important to me that I had earned the respect of my client and that my work spoke for itself.

By this time, my fixed salary (year-end bonus being significant and in addition) at Kotak had jumped from Rs 8 lakh to Rs 14 lakh, and then quickly to Rs 16 lakh on account of some industry movements. Morgan Stanley had made an entry into the market at the time, after its separation from JM Financial. Around the same time, Merrill Lynch had also become independent of DSP. Kotak, for obvious reasons, was the poaching ground for these companies. While many of my colleagues made the shift, I, however, didn't feel the need to do so. Not only was the money I was getting good,

Kotak was a good employer, where merit and not internal politics ruled the roost. In fact, at the end of the second year, on a Rs 16 lakh salary base, I earned Rs 32 lakh as bonus.

I remember calling my parents, who were over the moon to hear this. We couldn't help but recall how buying a builder floor worth Rs 32 lakh just four years earlier had been such a financial stretch. Now, I had earned exactly that amount as a single year's cash bonus.

Around July 2007, my sister, who was pursuing a course in actuarial science, got a job in Mumbai with Munich Re and moved in to live with us. While the one-BHK house was constricting for the three of us, we simply loved to have a family member staying with us after so long. In fact, her arrival brought home to us the fact that we were really missing our families. Even though her stay in Mumbai was short, the one incident from her stay that lives in my mind, albeit one that I am not very proud of, is a meeting with Shonak Sharma, an aspiring lawyer, whom she was dating at the time. In fact, she called Shonak home to introduce him to me. With all my proclamations about having a love marriage myself, I was far from the ideal brother when it came to my sister finding love. In fact, the only thing I remember saying to Shonak was a 'Hi' and a 'Bye'. Thankfully, that awkward meeting didn't come in the way, and Shonak is my brother-in-law now.

With my sister having received an offer from Max New York Life and moving back to Delhi shortly, we started missing home a lot more. That was when Madhuri and I decided that it was about time to start our own family. Soon, Madhuri was expecting, but she was in for a rough first trimester. In fact, on one of her visits to Panipat, to meet her parents, she had to be hospitalized. While I flew down to be with her, it was increasingly getting clear to us that staying in Mumbai was no longer a possibility and that we needed the support system of our family. Given Madhuri's condition, I applied for a transfer, informing the office of my personal commitments. Thankfully, Kotak was very accommodating, and by mid-2008 we had moved to Delhi.

Back Home

Our move back to Delhi was well timed to say the least. As they say, the markets are the only truth, and in 2008 the markets crashed. Mortgage crisis. Credit crisis. Government bailout. These were some of the phrases that would dominate news headlines in the months to come. The bankruptcy of Lehman Brothers on 15 September 2008, of course, marked the climax of the subprime mortgage crisis. Clearly, the glamorous phase of investment banking, as we'd known it all this while, was over.

In India we had seen early signs of the market going bust with the Reliance Power IPO, whose dream run on the stock exchange lasted all of a few minutes. Incidentally, this IPO was also being handled by Kotak. In fact, my boss, Sughosh Moharikar, was the point person from Kotak for the Anil Ambani Group. Their campaign 'Power On, India On' was the most marketed campaign that we had seen till date. Most people would still recall the illuminated balloons carrying their tagline all along Marine Drive, not to mention the high-decibel mass media campaign. When that IPO failed to perform, the markets tanked. Even before the IPO, we'd heard a cautionary voice from Sughosh, who'd admitted that this IPO was rather worrying. As he remarked, 'Reliance Power was at the time a company with one table and two chairs in Ballard Estate.' Of course, the Reliance Power IPO debacle went down in history as it wiped out many investors. In fact, Anil Ambani had to do a bonus issue of shares in which he didn't participate, to make good the losses incurred by the IPO investors. That the bear cycle had begun was clear for all to see.

My own earnings fell from Rs 48 lakh the year before to Rs 22 lakh that year. The joke in Kotak, in any case, was that the month of March always favoured Lala (Uday). Come appraisal time and either the quarter before the appraisal or the quarter in which the appraisal was being done became dry. These, of course, were unprecedented times.

Dust-Covered Police Jeeps

One of the deals that I was working on in 2008, before heading back to Delhi, was to do with HDIL. Owned by the Wadhawans, HDIL at the time wanted to take over a hotel chain called Six Senses. Launched by a Sindhi gentleman and his French girlfriend, Six Senses ran some extremely high-end sustainable luxury resorts and five-star hotels. Neeraj and I were assigned to the project. In fact, the two of us by now had become a strong team, having worked on several projects together.

My first visit to HDIL House in Bandra, however, had me thinking, '*Yahaan se zinda nikal gaye toh badi baat hai* (It will be a big deal if we are able to get out of here alive).' After parking my car in the basement, I was greeted with the sight of two police jeeps covered in dust. I had known that the Wadhawans had the reputation of being slumlords; in fact, their business model seemed to be: setting up slums, removing them, getting FSI (floor space index) and, in turn, selling it to other builders. The sight of the police jeeps gathering dust in their basement, however, was quite another thing.

Thankfully, the other clients that I had to work on weren't as colourful, though their deals were highly complex in their own right. One such complex deal had to do with the arbitrations between Indian telco Aircel's founder Sivasankaran and Malaysian operator Maxis Communications, on their $1.08 billion deal. While this deal had happened in 2006, at a later date Siva alleged that Maxis had deliberately denied him the earn-out on the deal by not going public timely and not making the EBITDA it could.

The dispute went under arbitration. It was at this time that Kotak was mandated to help Maxis prepare as the capital markets expert. This exposure allowed me to understand the telecom market in great depth. In fact, I had prepared an incisive report that was to be used by Maxis for the arbitration. Uday, however, refused to sign this report. He, with his instincts, had a whiff that this could lead to issues related to the allocation of 2G spectrum licences, and he wanted to steer clear of any controversy. While Maxis still used the report, it didn't go down as an official arbitration document. Uday's instincts turned out to be correct, of course, as the 2G scam was unearthed later. This was a $1 million fee mandate for Kotak, but clearly, he knew better: to let go of the immediate fee in favour of his reputation. In fact, one of the big learnings I have from Uday is that one must weigh the repercussions of one's involvement very carefully.

Close Shave with Death, a Major Personal Loss and Life Yet Again

While being stationed in Delhi, I had to travel to Mumbai to handle some of the deals that were in the works. Given my strong work ethic and the situation at the time, I made sure that I always stayed at my sister-in-law's place as opposed to a hotel. The fact that I was made to feel extremely welcome there by my sister-in-law and her husband, Deepak Gupta, made all the difference. While they had a one-BHK, they would gladly give the room to me, while they slept on the couch in the living room.

It was during one of my Mumbai visits that I had a narrow escape from death. It so happened that I thought I would give in to some gustatory pleasures while in the city. I called one of my childhood friends and neighbours from Malviya Nagar, Mansi Kohli, who was in Mumbai, to ask her and her husband to meet me for some famous chicken rolls at a joint called Khan Chacha in Colaba, located right behind the Taj hotel. At the last minute, though, Mansi got caught up in some official work and said that she would not be able to make it. By that time I was in a cab crossing the club grounds on Marine Drive towards Colaba. I soon received a call from my sister-in-law, asking me where I was; she told me that there seemed to be some news of a shootout in South Bombay and said that I should head to a safer location. Just like that, I took a U-turn from Chowpatty and headed to my colleague Shailesh Rathi's place in Dadar. Of course, by the time I reached there, all news channels were carrying the unbelievable news of the Taj hotel being under siege. Had fate not had bigger things lined up for me, I could have been right in the middle of the scene of death and destruction.

While my life had been spared, the big event that we were looking forward to as a family, the birth of our first child, was not to be. Madhuri's three-month ultrasound for foetal assessment revealed that there was an excess growth in the child's neck, pointing to the risk of the child being born with a disability. The news really shattered our world. While we were very sure that we would take care of the child come what may, thinking of the quality of life that the child would have eventually led us to the heartbreaking decision of having an abortion. It seemed like our world had come crashing down.

God, however, held our hand through this tough phase, as six months after this grim event, while on a trip to France and the US—which I had planned for Madhuri so she could put the past behind—she discovered that she was expecting again. We didn't, however, give ourselves the permission to be happy just yet, as the first three months were clearly a wait-and-watch. It was only after the first ultrasound that we could breathe easy. Our son, Avyukt Grover, was born on 5 February 2010, and he changed our world in a heartbeat. In fact, this was the one time that four generations of the Grovers—my grandfather (who lived till the ripe old age of ninety-six), my father, me and my son—lived in our Malviya Nagar home under the same roof. Life was indeed blessed again.

Challenging Assignments

On the work front, I continued to deliver my best and was part of several challenging assignments. The deal that I count among the most demanding had to do with the DLF–DAL merger. Prior to the DLF IPO, which had happened in 2007, the leased assets of the group had been bought over by the promoters and some investors, including Standard Chartered, in an entity called DLF Assets Ltd. There was, therefore, a significant revenue that had accrued prior to the IPO. In fact, this was also one of the reasons that the DLF IPO was very successful. In 2009, however, the real estate market started going through a slump. The DLF stocks, which were listed at over Rs 400 and had gone up to as much as Rs 1200 at one time, fell to nearly Rs 100 a share. One of the reasons for this was that the analyst community believed that the promoters should not own the leased assets outside the listed entity and that instead, all leased assets should lie within the group, as that's where a significant cash flow sits, and that cash flow should be used for developmental work.

In 2009, therefore, it was proposed that DLF Assets be merged with DLF Ltd. Meant to be a cashless transaction, it would give DLF shareholders a certain access to the merged entity while the promoters would increase their holding in the listed DLF Ltd. Since this was a related party transaction, three banks were appointed to lead the process, one of them being Kotak. Since I had cut my teeth in the real estate sector and was now based in Delhi, I was given the mandate. The big learning in this transaction came from dealing with some strong personalities, one of them being their CFO, Ramesh Sanka. In fact, I had to do a lot of pushback with Sanka, since his attempt was to structure the deal in a manner that would have favoured the promoters. At one point we even had shouting matches with the team in DLF. It reached such a pass that Sanka called my super boss, Falguni Nayar, to say that if your guy continued to create mayhem, they would take Kotak out of the deal. I was, however, proud that I had a voice, which I was using to be fair to the investors.

Structure-wise, this was one of the toughest deals to execute. DLF Assets had investments from DE Shaw and StanChart, who needed to exit and be offered a return on their money. In turn, the assets had to be brought into the listed company in a tax-efficient manner. I still recall the final board meeting where the merger was discussed at length. The chairman, Rajiv Singh, was extremely unhappy with the proposed merger ratio, so much so that he had raised his voice in the board meeting, forcing everyone else to slip into an uncomfortable silence. Once the merger ratio was frozen, the write-up to announce the deal to the stock market was also drafted on my computer, with Rajiv Singh and Cyril Shroff, from the law firm Amarchand & Mangaldas, in attendance.

Since I had executed this rather complex deal, my bosses became extremely confident of my abilities. In fact, post this deal, I also did a deal for the DLF family. This was to do with Pia Singh selling shares worth almost Rs 900 crore to her brother, Rajiv Singh. The deal was done at a price of Rs 240 per share, and it had to be executed as a block deal on the stock exchange. I remember going to Pia Singh's office in the evenings to inform her of the value of shares being sold the subsequent day. Given the confidence I had inspired, I would be the only person she would give the final sign-off to.

My real estate stint continued unabated as I also worked on the Bangalore-based Prestige Estate IPO. This was my fourth large real estate deal. Founded by a gentleman called Irfan Razack, the company had empanelled Merrill Lynch and Kotak for the job. I remember travelling extensively to Hong Kong with Irfan

Razack and their CEO for roadshows. On account of the trust that I inspired in the founder, when a meet to decide the anchor investors happened at the Oberoi Hotel at Nariman Point, with over twenty bankers and the IPO team in attendance, Mr Razack made it clear that while everyone could make their suggestions, it would be the list that would come from Ashneer's email ID that would be considered to be the final word.

The one thing that I think worked in my favour, not just with the Prestige Group but with all clients that I worked with, was the fact that I didn't sit in judgement over businesses. On the contrary, it was my solution-oriented approach that ensured that I offered some very specific resolutions to issues. It helped that I was exposed to a wide range of industries, which resulted in my incisive understanding of the overall market. Importantly, the deals that I handled weren't cookie-cutter deals, where, for example, one MNC was selling to another and therefore everything was pretty much in place. In executing an IPO, I nearly had to work as the company's CFO, ensuring that I problem-solved for the client. A case in point is the PC Jewellers IPO, which was managed by me end-to-end, from creating the pitch deck, benchmarking the brand against Tanishq or finally selling the story to investors. I did rounds of New York, Boston and San Francisco with the PCJ founder, Balram Garg, and pitched to investors there. Years later, when I went on to launch BharatPe, a lot of people lauded me for my fundraising abilities. It is a skill that has been honed over many such transactions.

Overall, what the stint at Kotak did for me was to boost my confidence tremendously, especially as I came face to face with successful founders. What I realized was that no one's business was perfect and that each of the founders had their own insecurities. While I looked up to these founders, I wasn't in awe of them. Instead, I realized how they had taken the right steps at the right time to be where they were. As I worked through the many deals along with global companies, such as Merrill Lynch, Citibank, Morgan Stanley and the like, my view always was that all of us were incidental and that the real game was being played by the promoters. I was, therefore, all the time, assimilating what the promoters had done to get to where they were. Growing up, in a middle-class service household, one had also been fed the biased view that businessmen must be making money out of malpractices, but I saw up close that the one thing the businessman was true to was his business.

Back home, I was also seeing Madhuri's business family pretty closely, and I realized how there was a difference in terms of the thought process of a service family versus a business family. While a service family was all about discipline and a certain routine, their ability to handle uncertainty was pretty limited. In my own household, I saw for a fact that Madhuri's ability to handle uncertainty as well as her aspirations in life were greater than I'd assumed. I was also beginning to realize that no one ever became rich by just earning a salary. In hindsight, it was here that the entrepreneurial bug had started to bite me. Somewhere within me I knew that if not now then at some point, entrepreneurship would be my calling.

A Plaque and a Five-Gram Gold Coin

It was an inside joke among my IIM batchmates that if you stayed in an organization long enough to earn gratuity, you were either unemployable elsewhere or you had mentally retired. I had already received a gratuity amount on completing five years at Kotak. The five-gram gold coin, and the ornamental plaque that came with it, spoke of years well spent in the organization. However, by 2013 I had started to get somewhat bored with the process. While I was doing enough deals, the cutting-edge action of investment banking of the early days was clearly waning. Not only were there more players, the fee was becoming thinner. Most clients had started to hire an M&A specialist in-house and were no longer happy giving a high success fee. Uday had also begun to feel that investment banking had become a practice as opposed to an institutionalized business. He was, therefore, less willing to offer equity for this business. Besides, my future at Kotak, if at all, lay in Mumbai, and the initial charm of the city had clearly worn off for me. I often tell people that in Mumbai, you start life in Borivali with the goal of moving to Bandra, then to Worli and finally to Nariman Point, and then you die. Essentially, your life's aspirations are reduced to having your first house in Borivali and your cremation in South Mumbai.

The fact that I was nearly the only person in my IIM batch who had done a stint longer than five years in an organization had also started to make me feel that perhaps I was settling down in a comfort zone and that it was time to explore other horizons.

It was at this time that my colleague Gesu Kaushal at Kotak put me in touch with her husband, Ajay. Ajay is the founder of BillDesk, one of those rare fintech companies that has been profitable and offered dividends to its investors. The company was to be acquired by PayU for $4.7 billion, in one of India's largest fintech deals. One thing led to another, and Ajay introduced me to Sanjay Rishi at American Express Bank, who was looking for someone to head corporate development (a fancy US name for investments and M&A) under him, and in his judgement my multi-industry experience worked well.

After a seven-year-long meaningful stint at Kotak, it was time to move on. I was very clear at the time that I wasn't going away from the Kotak way of life and the many valuable lessons that I had learnt there. Ironically, little did I know that Kotak would make an appearance in my later career, and an overly zealous faction would spin it into a whole new narrative.

Part 2: The AmEx Years

Gurgaon, 2013
American Sarkar Ki Naukri

The private joke at AmEx, when I joined, was to refer to our employment as 'American sarkar ki naukri'. I would soon figure out why. Working at AmEx was almost like being in a government job, a *sarkari naukri*, only in this case the sarkar was based in the US and spoke to us in dollars. My maiden stint at an MNC made me realize that MNC culture is far more relaxed than our home-grown 'Lala' companies. AmEx India was a huge set-up and had two sets of operations: (1) the back-office operations that supported the global business; and (2) the India-specific credit cards business, of which I was a part. It was a well-structured organization, and everyone had a well-defined role and slotted into established 'bands' or hierarchies. Your position in the different bands determined your salary and stock options, and therefore, everyone was aware of your 'aukaat'—your overall standing in the organization. I was a band 40. As for the work culture, the usual protocol was to conduct meetings, record their minutes and then follow up on them. To put it succinctly, *kahin koi aag nahi lagi thi*, there was no fire anywhere, including in most people's bellies.

Sanjay Rishi, my boss, however, was extremely aspirational. He was one of the first people who had worked in an MNC in India and had seen things progress from the days of the liberalization of the Indian economy, when corporate careers, as we know them today, were non-existent. Heading AmEx for South Asia, he was a career AmEx guy and understood the system extremely well. One of the youngest members of Sanjay's core CXO team, I was stationed right outside Sanjay's office and was seen by the rest of the organization as his blue-eyed boy.

AmEx was the third-largest credit card issuer in the country, and the big advantage it enjoyed was its end-to-end payment operation. It owned a unique bank licence, issued the cards, had its own network and also undertook merchant acquisition. While one-third of their business came from high-creditworthy individual consumers, the balance two-thirds came from companies, largely from the US-based MNCs. The problem at AmEx, however, was twofold. The first was the fact that, by design, they were very selective in whom they offered their card to—it was a luxury lifestyle payments brand as much as it was a utility service. And the second was that, despite the pitch to merchants that AmEx's ticket size was two times that of the market, the pace of merchant acquisition was restricted on account of the high commission (over 2.6 per cent) charged to them. This explains why when you enter a premium retail outlet, you will notice an 'AmEx Welcome' sticker on the outside, but the odds are that if you want to make the payment through an AmEx card, you will be told the machine is out of order. The merchant's hope in the process is that you will either dish out a VISA/Mastercard card, where he will have to pay a lower transaction fee, or, better still, that you will pay by cash. In the Indian market, where the margins in retail are dismal, the high transaction fee has been a big deterrent for AmEx. The AmEx market, therefore, has been largely restricted to hotels, airlines and high-end restaurants.

These challenges notwithstanding, in hindsight, that time was remarkable, as that was where I learnt end-to-end card economics, a learning that would come in handy in my later years, when I would set up BharatPe. The year I joined AmEx was also special for me on the personal front, since that was the year Madhuri and I were blessed with our second child, our daughter, Mannat. The year before, in 2012, Madhuri had conceived but by the third-month ultrasound, the same abnormality was seen in the foetus, and the pregnancy wasn't sustainable. We therefore had our fingers tightly crossed while expecting Mannat, and this time we were able to hold our bonny baby in our arms. With Avyukt and Mannat, our world was now complete, though we still carry the thought of having a third kid.

At work, my job was not to grow AmEx's traditional business but to evaluate the payment ecosystem and ascertain growth possibilities through minority investments in upcoming payments players. While the job wasn't too different from what I had done for so long, the payment space was a new ground for me. Early on in my assignment, I mapped the market fully to determine the key players, whether they were wallets, issuers, online payment aggregators or merchant acquirers. The one thing that I was constrained by were the numerous checks and balances placed on banks by the Fed privately in the aftermath of the 2008 crisis bailout. A private restriction placed on AmEx stated that acquiring more than 5 per cent equity in any company required a Fed approval. All the investments that I was exploring, therefore, needed to be minority investments.

Not deterred by this clause, I made it a point to meet every fintech founder personally. What worked in my favour was that each of these founders looked at AmEx's investment in their business as a validation of their business model, which was even more important than the cheque that would come their way.

Paytm and the Rebound MobiKwik Deal

As a part of my investment mandate, I had evaluated Paytm and the possibility of AmEx investing in it. This was before their famous Alibaba round. I had a long meeting with Vijay Shekhar Sharma. VSS was clearly a maverick founder and came across as a force of nature even in those early times. I simply loved the guy and the vision he had. We spent three long hours at the One97 Noida office, where he took me through the wallet story and explained how his ultimate vision was to build a digital currency. Having understood his vision, I invited VSS, along with his investment bankers, Madhur Deora (who is now their CFO) and Pankaj Jain from Citibank, to the AmEx office to make a pitch to my boss, Sanjay Rishi. Having arrived at the appointed hour, VSS pitched his investment deck to us. In between, he started to tell us that ICICI Bank and Mastercard had shown their intent in putting money into his venture. To Sanjay's surprise, he even proceeded to open his email on the projected screen and show us the ICICI proposal. I was all the time batting for VSS, given the fact that his business model was the future. That he was working at building a network, acquiring merchants and more, was a huge plus. In a lot of ways, what he was doing was very similar to what AmEx did, but at a mass scale, with mobile as the form factor, except here there was no need to underwrite any credit, as in this model people would load their own money in their wallets. Sanjay, however, comes from the old school of privacy and client confidentiality. In that one meeting, Sanjay had gauged that while this was a medium of the future, privacy wasn't VSS's forte, given his ICICI revelation to us. It would, therefore, be hard to sell him internally in the AmEx ecosystem, and culturally he wouldn't fit in.

While that deal didn't go through, having evaluated Paytm, we were clear that the future indeed lay in the wallet ecosystem. This, then, led us to move to the second-largest player, MobiKwik. AmEx eventually participated in the Series B round of MobiKwik. Technically, we were the lead investors in the round, having committed US$2.5 million. While Sequoia was already an investor in them, on AmEx's commitment of $2.5 million, Shailendra Singh spoke with me on the phone and agreed to put another $1 million. A larger Series B round got built subsequently, with Cisco and others participating.

Another company that I had evaluated and was trying to build a case for with Sanjay, while at AmEx, was Pine Labs. My thesis to Sanjay was that so far, the larger merchants had to put several different POS machines at the point of sale to optimize on the lower commission charged by banks on their own cards. Pine Labs, however, had developed a system where multiple acquiring banks could be configured at the back-end of a single POS card device. It was possible to set a rule at the back-end so that the transaction could hit the desired acquiring bank. I had the highest regard for Lokvir Kapoor, the founder of Pine Labs. An IIT alumnus, he had earlier worked overseas in Schlumberger, the energy services and equipment company, and had come back to India and built Pine Labs. What I personally liked about him was that he was a team player, so much so that he ensured that if he could live in upscale Vasant Vihar in Delhi, his core team could do the same. Lokvir had, however, diluted a substantial part of his equity, and at one time Sequoia Capital owned as much as 70 per cent stake in Pine Labs.

Besides the investment mandate that I had at AmEx, I also studied their balance sheet closely. I found that AmEx had taken a credit line from ICICI Bank at a 12 per cent interest rate. This led me to approach start-ups like Snapdeal, which were at the time raising huge funds from SoftBank. I convinced them to keep their treasury money in American Express Banking Corporation, which could earn them an interest rate of 9 per cent. By this arrangement, the AmEx cost reduced by as much as 3 per cent. While this wasn't a part of my mandate, I loved to unlock value wherever there was any opportunity.

Another great learning for me at AmEx was that nothing in life is cast in stone. AmEx globally had sold their banking business to Standard Chartered in 2008. Little did they realize that by virtue of that, their Indian banking licence would become defunct, as in India only licensed banks can issue credit cards. AmEx therefore reached a stalemate with RBI, wherein RBI wouldn't allow credit card issuance. It is folklore that AmEx then sent their master negotiator: a 'Jaat' Texan. The guy walked into the RBI office and said that either RBI had to make it work or they would be responsible for the loss of 15,000 jobs, as he would pack up AmEx from India and go back. AmEx today has a very unique banking licence in India, wherein they can't take public deposits and do not have to comply with priority sector lending requirements. The lesson that I learnt here: anything is possible as long as you negotiate hard. It came in very handy when, much later, I bought over PMC Bank from RBI at BharatPe.

Grofers Pitch Deck

Around the time I was closing the MobiKwik deal, I happened to meet one of my batchmates from IIT Delhi, Albinder Singh Dhindsa (Albi). At that time, he had quit Zomato and had just set up Grofers. I was quite taken by the name of his business, since it sounded like my last name, and I wanted to know what it was all about. 'It is a slang for a "mundu", a man Friday who can help with odds and ends,' Albinder explained. Essentially, at the time they were encouraging merchants not to keep their own delivery boys but to use Grofers' real-time delivery service that was available to them on an app, where they would be charged per delivery. Around this time, I had encouraged Madhuri to set up her own furnishings business from a small studio that we had set up in the basement of our home. Albi's app came in handy in her business and she ended up being one of the first few users of the Grofers B2B delivery service.

I was approached by Albinder again in January 2015. By that time, he had already run the service for a few months and had raised $0.5 million seed round from Sequoia. This time he wanted me to help him create a formal pitch deck for Grofers' consumer-facing grocery delivery business and help raise funds. Having consumed so many pitch decks on the other side,

I readily agreed to help him. Interestingly, the pitch deck of Grofers was made in the AmEx office. My work for the day done, at around 9 p.m., Albinder would come to the AmEx office, and we would sit in the meeting room and work on the pitch deck. I also connected him with VCs, and we raised US$10 million in the Series A. The money raised, Albinder called me for a meeting to thank me for all the help that I had rendered. This was followed up with a proposal: 'Why don't you join Grofers?' I had been exposed to the entrepreneurial space long enough by the time and had begun to see that most founders had similar educational qualifications as me, and some of them had even worked for fewer years, which would mean they would have lesser money as a safety net while taking the plunge. This gave me a lot of confidence.

As I made Rs 80 lakh (US$110,000) as the annual salary at the time at AmEx, Albinder mentioned that, those being early times at Grofers, they couldn't afford me at that salary, but that he could offer Rs 40 lakh (US$55,000) as fixed salary and would initially issue ESOPs for the balance Rs 40 lakh. This was roughly at $35 million post-money valuation at the time. I tend to be an instinctive decision-maker, and I trust people rather quickly; and this, of course, was a former batchmate. Just like that, I agreed to Albi's offer. At that time, Flipkart had touched a valuation of $8 billion. My ask to Albinder was that if I delivered Grofers a valuation of US$8 billion, I should be able to earn Rs 100 crore (US$15 million) for myself; in hindsight, Rs 100 crore was perhaps the largest figure I could think of at the time. Albi agreed, we shook hands on the promise, and here I was, ready to jump on to the start-up bandwagon.

When my boss Sanjay Rishi heard of my decision, he was sceptical to say the least. From his perspective, leaving the stability of AmEx for an unheard-of company, whose office was a small warehouse and whose staff strength was some fifteen-odd people, didn't make too much sense. However, seeing my resolve, he knew better than to try to hold me back. With an open offer to join AmEx at any time should I feel the need, I bid adieu to my corporate years.

5

Grofers: The Beginning of My Entrepreneurial Journey

Gurgaon, 2015

'Anticipatory Bail'

That was the name of the first-ever file I created on my new Apple computer, on Day 1 of joining Grofers as their CFO.

Operating out of a small warehouse in Gurgaon with fifteen-odd people, Grofers had just about pivoted from being a B2B brand offering delivery services to merchants to a consumer-facing brand delivering groceries and doing at best thirty orders a day.

'We had a good day yesterday, with a total of thirty orders, but *ek panga ho gaya* (there has been a problem),' I was informed by Albinder on the first day of my joining. Apparently, Grofers had onboarded an organic vegetable vendor. This guy, one Mr Kapoor, ended up ordering vegetables worth Rs 500 from his own organic vegetable business listed on Grofers, to be delivered to his own house. It so happened that with thirty-odd orders to fulfil on the day, the manager overlooked the fact that the order was for organic veggies and ended up sending veggies from a regular vendor and fulfilling the order. Kapoor was infuriated and saw it not as an instance of wrong delivery but as a case of fraud. So much so that he registered a case with the neighbouring Greater Kailash police station. As luck would have it, Kapoor lived in the same compound as Arun Jaitley, the then finance minister. Since his address was the same as the minister's, the police station didn't waste any time in officially lodging his complaint. A case under Section 420 of the Indian Penal Code was therefore registered against the two directors of Grofers, Albinder Singh Dhindsa and his co-founder Saurabh Kumar, for alleged cheating.

Albinder wanted me to take up this matter and help resolve it. My brother-in-law, Shonak, is a criminal defence lawyer, and hence, he was my go-to person in this case. He was quick to get Albinder and Saurabh anticipatory bail from the Saket Court. While this was a relief, it technically only meant that the police would inform them seven days in advance of making any arrest. The issue still needed resolution. I tried to reason it out with Kapoor but soon realized that his angst ran deeper and that it wasn't just about being delivered the wrong veggies. His son had apparently set up a company called I Say Organic, and despite the fact that it had started much before Grofers, it had failed to garner investor interest. Now that he had to reconcile to being a vendor with Grofers, he didn't take to it very kindly. It was clear that he wouldn't let the matter go so easily.

Since an FIR had been filed, it could be quashed only by the high court. Shonak put me in touch with a high court lawyer who had a practice in Niti Bagh, Delhi. A jolly, Punju lawyer, he assured me in his Punjabi accent that it was too minor a case and that he would have it quashed. To my queries, on whether he needed any other details, his reply was a relaxed, '*Grover saab ji, chaddo mitti pao, main rafa dafa karva dena hai* (I will have it taken care of).' But he was either ill-prepared or overconfident.

On the allotted date, the high court refused to quash the FIR. For the first time in my career, I felt like I had let down someone who had placed his confidence in me. Albinder, however, quickly put me in touch with Giri Subramanium, the son of Gopal Subramanium. Subramanium senior, of course, besides being a lawyer of repute, has served as the solicitor general of India. On Giri's advice, we assigned the case to another senior lawyer, one Mr Sethi. The strategy was that we would put up the case once again before the high court, for it to be rejected. That rejection, in turn, would pave the way for us to move to the Supreme Court. As planned, the case for quashing the FIR was put up for hearing one more time and was rejected yet another time, enabling us to knock on the door of the Supreme Court.

At this stage, I requested Giri if we could ask his father to represent us in the Supreme Court. Back in the day, senior lawyers of his standing charged as much as Rs 7.5 lakh per hearing. It was a huge amount to pay, but we simply couldn't afford to take any risks.

I recall my meeting with the distinguished lawyer Gopal Subramanium vividly. After I had explained the case to him, his response was fifteen minutes of hysterical laughter. He found it hard to believe that a case of this nature was being taken to the Supreme Court. One question that he did ask me, once he'd stopped laughing at the absurdity of the case, was the name of the judge in whose court the hearing was slated to take place. When I replied that it would be Jagdish Singh Khehar (who later went on to become the forty-fourth chief justice of India), he did caution me that the case could go either way.

On the appointed date, we were at the highest court of the land for a case that involved vegetables worth Rs 500 and had seen multiple high court hearings. Our case was listed at number 14. Fourteen is my birthdate and my lucky number, and I really hoped to God that it would prove to turn lucky that day. To be honest, though, it didn't seem like a possibility, especially as the first thirteen cases listed ahead of us met with a firm dismissal in all of two minutes.

After every case number was called out, there were two distinct sounds that I heard—'Janab', by way of attempted explanation from the defendant's lawyer, followed by a thud made by the case file having been dropped by the judge, indicative of the case's dismissal. Clearly, this Rs 500 case had become an albatross around my neck.

The call for case number 14, however, wasn't followed by the customary 'Janab'. Instead, Gopal Subramanium opened with an assertion that caught the attention of the judge: 'This is the most interesting case of my career,' he stated with a flourish. He followed this up with an analogy. 'Sir, a streetside vendor sold you a mango, claiming that it was sweet. You ate the mango and didn't find it sweet. Will our judicial system allow itself to be clogged by such cases?' He quickly went on to explain that if the gentleman under question was claiming that he was defrauded, we had to be able to see the property under question to determine if it was indeed a case of fraud. Essentially, he used a technical argument to draw attention to the fact that the police hadn't preserved the property, the vegetables in this case. Importantly, he was clear that at the level of the Supreme Court, the verdict had to be based on the interpretation of the law and not just on the merit of the case. He was right. To the fact that there was no property, which could prove whether the vegetables were organic and therefore whether defrauding had indeed happened, the judge noted his agreement. The FIR was summarily quashed and the case dismissed.

It is another matter that we had to spend eighteen long months fighting a Rs 500 case while also spending over Rs 25 lakh to resolve it. Interestingly, in this intervening period of eighteen months, every single fundraising meeting that I set up had to begin with an explanation of this curious case, u/s 420 ('char sau beesi'), on the Grofers founders.

* * *

The responsibility at Grofers was divided in a manner that product and tech were handled by Albinder, operations were overseen by Saurabh, while everything that was commercial, regulatory and financial was under my purview. While I was designated as the CFO, I had stepped into the shoes of the third co-founder from Day 1 of my joining.

Besides handling the odd case of Mr Kapoor and the veggies, the first nine months at Grofers went by in a flurry of activity for me. On the one hand we were expanding to a new city every week, while on the other there were a series of fundraising rounds. While the Series A round had seen participation from Tiger and Sequoia, with $5 million each at a valuation of $35 million, the Series B financing round saw Tiger, Sequoia as well as the DST Group (participating through another investing entity called Apolletto). I thereafter initiated the Series C round, in which we saw not just these investors but also SoftBank joining hands for a total funding of $120 million. Albi and I were a strong team. When it came to going to the US for fundraising, Albi preferred to do it himself, but once the term sheets were signed, I would solely take over till the money hit our account.

The year 2015 was truly the year of Grofers, as we went from a valuation of $35 million to $370 million in a matter of nine months. Our biggest competitor at the time was Bigbasket. However, so deft were Albi and I as a team in terms of fundraising that we caught them unawares. This, despite the fact that Bigbasket had a business that was twice as big as ours. They also had better sourcing capabilities than us and hence had better margins. However, they were old school, and their tech particularly was poorer. Come to think of it, Grofers and Bigbasket had complementary skills. If they knew retail well, we were great at tech and digital marketing. If they were smart in warehousing, we were great at last-mile delivery. If they were big in south India, we were big in the north. It was a typical Zomato–Swiggy story, only in this case, while we were raising funds in quick succession, Bigbasket wasn't able to do it.

Between the Series A and Series B rounds, Albinder also wanted me to flip the company to a new jurisdiction—in this case, to Singapore. There were several reasons for this, and contrary to popular perception, tax saving wasn't one of them. The first was that if the company was based out of India, investors were loath to sit on the board of directors for fear of being dragged into such Rs 500 cases, as in India there is no difference in law between an executive director and other directors in terms of culpability. Anyone filing any case against the company simply had to pick up the names of the directors of the company from the Registrar of Companies. There was also more flexibility in Singapore when it came to structuring the shareholding agreement in terms of preference shares and debentures as opposed to simple equity. Besides, with the risk of frequent unpredictable changes in FDI restrictions in multi-brand retail in India, Flipkart had been externalized to Singapore in 2011. Albi felt that if there was, at a later date, any possibility of a merger with them, it could be done with fewer complications if Grofers was also externalized.

Through mutual contacts, I was led to a tax expert, Harshal Kamdar, who worked at PwC at the time. An extremely sorted guy when it came to taxation and structuring, he had done a couple of these externalizations. With his inputs, we created a company in Singapore with a mirror-shareholding structure as the Indian entity. All shareholders then subscribed to Grofers International Pte Ltd shares at nominal value. The one challenge that I had was to do with the shares of Deepinder Goyal of

Zomato, who had invested Rs 60 lakh in Grofers. While the rest of the shareholders had earned money outside India, and had foreign accounts and could transfer funds from their foreign accounts, the same wasn't true of Goyal. The challenge, therefore, lay in the allocation of shares to him. Until we got Albinder's relative who was a US resident to subscribe to the shares and then make a gift deed to Deepinder.

The Singapore entity thus created was christened Grofers International Private Limited, while Grofers India was now its subsidiary. It was a complicated transition, especially as we had to endorse thousands of agreements that had been entered into with small shopkeepers. I completed the entire process in under two months.

Naivety

'Is Albinder's heart in the right place?'

I was taken aback to hear Madhuri raise this question to me. This was at a time when, post the Series D funding round, Albinder and Saurabh did secondary sales of their shares that offered them liquidity. Both he and Saurabh bought Range Rovers—in fact, Madhuri's family got them a sweet deal from Karnal. The original team that had been in place before my joining was also given BMWs in recognition of their efforts. For the first time, I had stopped in my tracks to see that despite all the heavy-lifting that I had done, I was yet to see any monetary gains for myself. My shares, of course, hadn't vested by then, so there was no opportunity to sell. I was, however, enjoying work too much to allow this setback to come in my way. Besides, I trusted the guy.

Madhuri, however, being her perceptive self, felt that Albinder had failed to acknowledge my role in the 10x growth that the company had achieved since my joining. Much later, I also realized that Albinder was getting new people to join in, who weren't even CXOs, at salaries in crores, while I continued to draw my original salary of Rs 40 lakh.

It was only in June 2016 that I decided to have a heart-to-heart conversation with Albinder and asked him point-blank if there was a problem. 'Why are you saying this?' went his reply. I reminded him that while I was the CFO of a company worth $350 million, my salary was as low as Rs 40 lakh. An apology followed, with an innocuous explanation that it had escaped his notice and that I should go ahead and revise my salary. As a CFO, focused as I was to keep company expenses under check, I went on to revise my salary to Rs 75 lakh, still short of the original salary of Rs 80 lakh at AmEx. My ESOPs were still not revised, as Albi didn't feel it was the right time to approach investors with this proposal. In hindsight, it was my naivety that prompted me to take things at face value.

While my financial growth was stunted, in terms of business we had progressed from thirty orders a day to 30,000 orders a day and had a footprint in thirty cities. From a small warehouse, where we had begun our journey, we had now moved to a 50,000-square-foot office, one that I had helped put together. In fact, in my bid to get speedy work done at low cost, I had involved Madhuri in the project, who was now diversifying from her furnishings business and taking up turnkey projects. This project, of course, was done by her on a no-profit-no-loss basis. We turned around the office from scratch in three months and in under Rs 1.5 crore (at less than Rs 300/sq. ft). In fact, Kalyan Krishnamurthy of Tiger Global, who was one of our investors, happened to visit our new office at the time. They had recently done up a 30,000-square-foot office for Tiger Global in Bangalore, which had a cricket pitch with retractable nets. 'How much did doing up this office cost you?' he asked me out of curiosity, given his own newly done-up office. On hearing that it had cost Rs 1.5 crore, he further inquired if I was telling him the entire amount or just the GST figure. Turns out that Tiger had spent Rs 12 crore doing up their office, and the amount that we had spent would perhaps not even add up to the GST figure that they had paid. That it spoke strongly of our cost-control mechanisms was clear for all.

Madhuri, of course, went on to take up other projects after this, an interesting one being doing up a farmhouse for Rahul Sharma of Micromax. That project had come about so well, as she told me, that I couldn't stop myself from going and seeing it. Posing as Madhuri's man Friday who had come to drop off her stuff, I was literally blown away on seeing the place, which even had a golf course inside. This was later to become the Bollywood actress Asin's home. But I digress.

As far as the Grofers business model went, along the way we pivoted from the marketplace model, where we didn't stock any inventory, to having our own dark stores. The big disadvantage with the marketplace model was that the inventory of the shopkeepers wasn't live. Every so often, having received an order, when our field agent went to pick up the order from the shop, he would receive only part products. This not only caused huge operational issues, it also led to major discord with the customers. The regulations, however, didn't allow a foreign-owned entity to carry out retail business in India, and the e-commerce regulations were yet to see the light of day. I, therefore, worked at putting together an FDI-compliant structure that would enable us to own inventory and conduct business. For this, I created another subsidiary of the Singapore holding company called Hands on Trade (HOT). I also put together a few Indian-owned intermediate companies, so that when an order was placed on Grofers India, HOT, the wholesale entity, would sell to the intermediate entity, and, in turn, the intermediate entity would issue the invoice to the customer. Not only did I create this structure, it also became a template for other e-commerce players like Amazon. Later, when the government allowed 100 per cent foreign-owned companies to carry out food retail through a licence, I also ensured that Grofers became the first foreign entity to be issued this licence.

The Proposed Grofers–Bigbasket Merger

By mid-2016, the Grofers business had started stagnating. While we did business of $3–4 million every month, the burn was as much as $4–5 million a month. The year 2016 was also when Flipkart was going through a tough time with the Snapdeal–Flipkart deal going on and off, and the overall funding scenario was becoming tighter. By January 2017, SoftBank, which had burnt its hands in Snapdeal, started to get jittery. With Nikesh Arora, the president of SoftBank, moving on, Grofers was tagged as a Nikesh legacy company within the SoftBank ranks. I realized that SoftBank would not put any additional money into such a scenario. It was then that I suggested to Vikas Parekh, my counterpart at SoftBank (who worked, years later, closely with Masa San on WeWork), that we should attempt a Grofers–Bigbasket merger. The last funding round that Bigbasket had raised was with the Qatar Investment Authority. Clearly, since they had gone up to the sovereign fund, there weren't many other avenues left for them to explore. As a combined entity, however, I felt that we could easily command a billion-dollar valuation. I worked on the project in detail from March through July 2017, including on the likely valuation ratios for both the companies. There were, however, other external factors at play that would soon come in the way.

Alibaba-backed Paytm had set up the Paytm Mall in February 2017, a B2C model inspired by China's TMall, and had ended up burning a lot of money in the process. They were under tremendous pressure and were looking at strengthening their play in the e-commerce space. To them, Bigbasket seemed an investment that

could help them strengthen their online-to-offline strategy. The
Paytm Mall–Bigbasket deal eventually went through, with Paytm
Mall picking up a 40 per cent stake in Bigbasket. All thanks to
Madhur Deora, who had by then joined Paytm as its CFO and
knew Bigbasket well, as Citi was their investment banker.

Once that avenue was shut, I knew we didn't have a fighting
chance. More than anything else, as a CFO, the pain of losing
money on every single order was hard for me to disregard. While our
average order size was between Rs 1000 to Rs 1200, our earnings net
of discounts on such orders was Rs 120, whereas last-mile delivery
itself cost us Rs 150. I was closer than anyone else to the real situation
and knew that the Grofers growth story wasn't sustainable.

Parting Ways

Once growth stagnated, there were frequent tiffs between Albi and
Saurabh. One reason for this was the fact that the people Saurabh
had appointed, largely from his alma mater, proved to be quite
subpar. Albi knew of it. I had myself had a run-in with these guys
on several occasions, and I strongly felt that the company hadn't
invested in quality manpower. Each time, however, I would make
a point with Saurabh's recruits, he looked at it as an invasion of
his authority, till one day he put his foot down with Albi and said
that I should be asked to go.

Oberoi Hotel, Gurgaon, was the venue of the final meeting
between Albi and me, where he suggested it was time for us to
part ways. While I did not contest that as I wasn't a believer in the
Grofers growth story any more, I was clear that after working for
two and a half years and having led the company to that valuation,
I needed to be compensated for my efforts. But the equity that I
actually held as ESOPs was too low—a mere Rs 2.4 crore at the
latest valuation. Of that, too, only about 30 per cent of the ESOPs
had actually vested.

My initial conversation with Albi was that our original handshake was for Rs 100 crore at a valuation of $8 billion. Even if I did a quick math, at a valuation of $370 million, I should have been holding at least Rs 10 crore of equity. In all fairness, I therefore asked that I be offered Rs 1 crore as a settlement amount. Albi, however, wasn't keen to offer even this amount and tried to negotiate with me. While I had great respect for Albi as a founder, and I remain friends with him, at that point, however, I felt that I was being handed the short end of the stick, given my contribution to Grofers. Several years later, a number of Grofers employees would go on to join me at BharatPe, a validation of the value that I had added to Grofers.

While I had joined Grofers with a lot of enthusiasm for the start-up world, my exit was far from amicable. When I realized that I wasn't being offered a fair deal, left with no other choice, I had to block a few bank accounts to bring Albi to the table. I couldn't make peace with the fact that the back-breaking work I had put in was being devalued to this extent. More than the money, I couldn't reconcile with the fact that I had been taken completely for a ride. I now saw my wife's prophecy, that I was being too trusting for my own well-being, coming true.

Pushed to a corner, Grofers did offer the settlement amount of Rs 1 crore, and I came out of the Grofers stint totally broken and was left questioning my own instincts. Little did I know at the time that I was to go down in history as perhaps the lone start-up founder who would be shortchanged twice.

Interestingly, it was at Grofers—in a conversation with Kotak CEO Deepak Gupta at our Sector 32, Gurgaon, office—that I had first mentioned the need for a single QR for shopkeepers. Little did I know that after one stint I would land up building a large business around the concept.

6

A Dark Phase

'There are two buses. One reaches your bus stop first but thereafter, reaches your destination late; the other reaches your bus stop later but makes you reach your destination earlier than the first bus. If you belong to the service class, you will end up taking the first bus, as you would rather be on the path, i.e., doing something all the time.'

I had heard an ex-boss tell this story often as an example of how people have an activity orientation without thinking through the meaningfulness of the activity. Little did I know that one day I would be struggling with this dilemma myself. For the first time in my career, I had left, or rather had been asked to leave, a place, and I hadn't landed at a better place, something that can create a big dent in one's self-worth. What added to my stress was to see my father worrying incessantly and being highly insecure about my being out of a job. 'Did you do anything wrong that Albinder had to ask you to leave?' This question, from my dad particularly, had me in the throes of despair.

In my heart I knew that I wanted to take the entrepreneurial route. At this stage, however, sheer exhaustion had got the better of me. In the last two and a half years I had taken on too much and had solved far too many problems. I finally decided to take time to board the proverbial second bus, and to use the intervening time to meet people and figure out my path.

The obvious people to touch base with were my batchmates who had turned entrepreneurs, only to realize that not many were forthcoming with any support. One of my early meetings was with Anshoo Sharma, who had set up Magicpin, an app that aids discovery of local businesses. While I spent some time in his office understanding his business, the conversation was fleeting, as I didn't see any real interest from him in forging a partnership with me. Yet another set of discussions happened with my IIT and IIM batchmate Nitin Gupta, the founder of PayU India, a payment service provider.

Nitin himself has a spectacular story. One of those smart people who had cracked the 'Day Zero', Rs 1-crore placement at IIM, he went on to join Lehman Brothers. Along the way, he co-founded a company called Khoj Guru, a great product for local search. While he continued working at Lehman, he would send money to two of his schoolmates who ran the entrepreneurial venture. A believer in the 'too big to fail' doctrine, at the brink of the Lehman crash, he invested all his savings in buying Lehman stock. With Lehman's fall from grace came his own insolvency. As he turned his attention to Khoj Guru post the debacle, it turned out that his co-founders weren't happy having him on board. He had turned risk-averse after losing all his money and chose to take on the Naspers model of entrepreneurship, where he was offered the designation of a founder but with phantom equity. What the Naspers model essentially means for an entrepreneur is that he acts as a hired founder without fundraising responsibilities and typically with a 5 per cent uptake. It is on this model that he and Shailaz Nag built PayU India, which has since grown to be a leading online payment provider. In fact, while at Grofers, I had many interactions with Nitin. Nothing, however, came out of our entrepreneurial brainstorming sessions. Subsequently, Nitin abruptly left when PayU bought over Citrus, and brought in Jitendra Gupta and Amrish Rau as its management team.

Disillusioned with the lack of any progress in the entrepreneurial space, I turned my attention to the job market once again, only to meet further disappointment there as well. I was reminded of the open offer that my boss at AmEx, Sanjay Rishi, had given to me when I had quit. Sanjay, however, by this time had moved to the US as a part of AmEx's M&A team and wasn't as powerful within the system. Although he did put me in touch with the AmEx Ventures team, that conversation didn't take off. By that time, Kalyan Krishnamurthy of Tiger Global had joined Flipkart. A meeting with his right-hand man, for a deputy CFO role at Flipkart, didn't fructify either.

To say that I was disheartened would be an understatement. Having worked as the youngest CFO of a start-up and having built a company to ten times its value, it was ironic that businesses weren't taking advantage of my competencies. Shorn of options, I decided to turn to investment banking, the genesis of my career.

A Fifteen-Minute Stint

It was at this time that I spoke to Prashant Singhal, a distinguished corporate professional and a partner at Ernst & Young, who then put me in touch with his M&A team. Given the vibrant start-up culture, E&Y was expecting its start-up practice to scale and saw a lot of merit in my experience. Convinced that I had a ringside view of the space and also spoke the language of start-ups, E&Y made me an offer. While the salary on offer was Rs 1 crore, my only pain point was that they weren't offering me a position as a 'partner'. However, on their assurance that I would get to the partner position within six months, I decided to take the offer.

Walking into the Aerocity office of E&Y, I was filled with a sinking feeling in the pit of my stomach. I found myself staring at people in dark suits, looking as grim as ever. While some were sitting behind glass walls, the others veritably junior to them in the hierarchy had workstations outside. A deathly silence permeated the office. Unnervingly, I could feel a choking sensation rising in my chest, almost as if I would have a heart attack.

No sooner was I called into the cabin of my reporting manager than I blurted out, '*Sir, galti ho gayi* (I have made a mistake).' I confessed to him that the environment was making me choke. Knowing that I came from the start-up space, he understood my predicament and asked me not to take any impulsive decision. I, however, called Prashant Singhal and profusely apologized to him; while I was grateful that he had initiated me into the place, for the life of me I couldn't acclimatize to it. '*Mujhe andar se awaaz aa rahi hai ki mera corporate career khatam ho chuka hai* (An inner voice tells me that my corporate stint is over),' I confessed. That call made, I came out of the E&Y office, having spent all of fifteen minutes that seemed like a lifetime. My first communication on stepping out was to my dad, to tell him that I was certain that I would die if I had to work in such an environment. He had sensed my desperation, and his advice to me was a hugely relieving 'follow your heart'. Thus ended my corporate stint, one that had set some sort of a record in terms of being the shortest stint in corporate history.

* * *

Karol Bagh, November 2017

Around the time the E&Y assignment had come up, I had reconnected with Balram Garg, the owner of PC Jewellers. I had worked with him closely during my stint at Kotak Investment Banking, helping him go public through a successful IPO. Balram

Garg was keen that I join him. I was a bit sceptical, though, of working with a 'Lala'. His shop, based in Karol Bagh, a place known for its budget shopping, seemed far removed from the places I had worked at so far. However, given my last corporate experience, I knew I had to be open to possibilities. True to my basic skill of unlocking value, what excited me about his offer was that he wanted to build a whole new gold loan vertical. I wasn't sure, however, if he would be ready to offer decent remuneration. To his 'let me know what you are looking for', I asked for a salary of Rs 1 crore with stock options. His counteroffer was an acceptable Rs 85 lakh as fixed salary and Rs 3 crore in stocks.

While I was happy with the offer, my family was cynical of my move from the posh office of E&Y in Aerocity to the streets of Karol Bagh. What worked for me was that I saw intrinsic value in his proposed gold loan business. To my mind, viability and not just valuation was an important aspect of running a business. As a matter of fact, the one thing that bothered me at Grofers was that the business per se wasn't profitable. Post my exit, a down round reducing Grofers's valuation was a vindication of my lack of belief in the fundamentals of that business. In fact, the Grofers valuation increase in all these years has been equivalent to the cash infusion into the business as opposed to any tangible value creation. I wanted to now learn from a Baniya Lala how to create a profitable business using customers.

My decision made, the daily drives to Karol Bagh began. It was a struggle to find parking space every morning in the bylanes of the shopping hub. That Herculean task accomplished, I would make an entry through the glittering showroom of PC Jewellers, step out into the back lane and get into an unoccupied office that seated me and Nikhilesh Govil, an ex-colleague from Kotak, who ran their online business.

Once at work, the familiar ritual of creating a business plan, this time for a gold loan business, kept me in high spirits. I studied the market thoroughly, including the business models of Muthoot and the Manappuram Group. Around this time, a gentleman called Sumit Maniyar was launching Rupeek, a fintech based out of Bengaluru, focused on branchless online gold loan business. 'You are the one person who gets what I am trying to build,' he said at the end of our meeting—as much an endorsement for him as it was for me, new as I was to the sector.

Besides trying to set up PCJ's gold loan business, I ensured that their core jewellery retail business was digitized, even if it was not a part of my mandate. This meant putting Paytm and PhonePe QRs at their shops. Additionally, having seen the issues faced in reconciliation between the shop sales and their central accounts teams, I also replaced the many different card acceptance machines they used for various banks with a Pine Labs POS that could, at the back-end, collate transactions across acquiring banks. I also digitized their gift card with Qwikcilver Solutions (acquired by Pine Labs later) and also their deposit scheme business. Balram Garg loved my initiative and the fact that I wasn't restricted by my job description.

At this time, the PC Jewellers stock was trading at an all-time high of Rs 400. Balram Garg wanted to up his game and apply for an NBFC licence for the gold loan business. Little did we know that the world order as we knew it then was about to change irreversibly.

'PNB fraud: CBI seeks Interpol help, notice against Nirav Modi, others issued', *India Today*, 16 February 2018.
'How Nirav Modi Pulled Off the Great Indian Bank Robbery', *Mint*, 23 February 2018.

Thus ran the headlines of most dailies as the Nirav Modi scam was beginning to be unearthed. With the diamantaire leaving a $1.8-billion hole in PNB's books, it was a natural corollary that all jewellery stocks with the exception of Tanishq began their free fall. To make matters worse, banks took a call that all credit lines to jewellers needed to be pulled back. For the first time I saw Balram Garg under tremendous stress. Although gold inventory is one of the safest inventories, his additional issue was that a lot of his money was stuck in exports to Dubai, with receivables not being realized. The market quickly started losing faith in the PCJ stock. I recall how I had to step in with a number of investor calls to convince them that our business was here to stay. Internally, however, I had begun to realize that this was now a game of survival.

In June 2018, I had a meeting with Balram Garg to inform him that I wouldn't be able to continue with PCJ. He, however, wanted me to give him some time, since he didn't want the market to perceive that his core team was exiting. I honoured his request. There was no way I could forget that at the time of my exit from Grofers, neither my batchmates nor my ex-bosses could do anything for me. If there were two people who had stood by me, they were Prashant Singhal of E&Y and Balram Garg of PCJ. For both, I have the highest regard.

While most people view my PCJ stint as a step back in my career trajectory, it is my firm belief that if I hadn't taken those few steps allegedly backwards, I wouldn't have been able to dart ahead with BharatPe. I say this for several reasons. Firstly, *dukandar wali kahani PCJ se shuru hui thi*—it was at PCJ that I understood the problem statement of a shopkeeper and the mentality of a Baniya businessman, and hence the final pieces of the BharatPe puzzle had miraculously come together. Besides, had I joined any other place, my opportunity cost to leave would have been extremely high. At the end of the PCJ stint, however, I had zero opportunity cost, especially as my stock had come to nothing. I could therefore easily move on to explore other avenues when they presented themselves.

7

BharatPe: The Genesis

Vipin Agarwal: 'We are funding an early-stage fintech for which we are looking for a CEO. In case you know of anyone who could be interested, do connect.'

Having made my decision to move on known to Balram Garg, I was thinking of the road ahead when this message on my IIM Ahmedabad WhatsApp group caught my attention. I knew that Agarwal worked for Fosun, a Chinese fund. Why would an early-stage investment need a CEO? I couldn't wrap my head around this. Keen to find out more, I texted back asking to be connected, more out of intrigue than anything else.

A hot Sunday afternoon, sometime in June 2018, was when I was scheduled to meet Bhavik Koladiya, of the said fintech. We had agreed to meet at the IIT Delhi campus, and I had told Madhuri that she could expect me back latest in an hour. But the meeting lasted over four hours. I learnt that Bhavik Koladiya and Shashvat Nakrani were originally from Bhavnagar, Gujarat. The two went back a long way, as Bhavik had studied under Shashvat's dad, Mansukhbhai Nakrani, who ran a school and an engineering college in Bhavnagar. While Shashvat had just about completed his third year of engineering at IIT Delhi, Bhavik, 5–6 years older, was staying at the IIT hostel along with him. With three other guys under their wing—Satyam, Tanmay and Yogi, also IIT Delhi students—they had collectively participated in and won a UPI hackathon.

For the next hour or so, Bhavik explained to me how all UPI payment apps could run on a single QR, an idea that I had seen merit in during my stint at Grofers. In Bhavik, however, I found a technical viability of this idea as he explained that in UPI architecture, money transfer, whether it is from one customer to another or from a customer to a merchant, works on the same principle, as technically it is a bank-to-bank transfer. At the time, the existing payment apps, Paytm and PhonePe, were charging merchants a fee of 2 per cent per transaction. Bhavik's idea was to reduce the charge to 1 per cent and get these merchants into their fold.

'You are only playing on the arbitrage and doing nothing game-changing then,' was my immediate reaction to Bhavik. For the next few minutes, we ended up playing a Q&A game.

Bhavik: 'Isn't that how the market works?'

Me: 'If architecturally, P2P and P2M have the same architecture in UPI, over time the cost of merchant transactions will become zero, like for consumer transfers. Cost becoming zero, competitive pressure will force someone else to reduce the charge from 1 per cent to 0.9 per cent, and thereon it will only be a game of who can drop the rates faster.'

Bhavik: 'How else do we make a business out of it?'

Me: 'The only way this business can become big is through distribution and not selling.'

Bhavik: 'What do you mean?'

Me: 'You can make the service free, so that there is wide acceptance and all that is required of us is to send an agent to the merchant to onboard him.'

In a matter of minutes, Bhavik realized that while technologically they were on to something, for building a business they needed someone like me at the helm of things from the very start, as a co-founder. I understood from Bhavik that they had just set up the company, two-odd months ago, and so far they had put in a total of Rs 1 lakh as initial share capital between him and Shashvat, with no business. At some point they had met Fosun, who had agreed to incubate them and was now talking about giving them $250,000 for a 25 per cent stake in the company. However, even though they had been sitting at the Fosun office for the last three months, nothing had really moved.

Credit Card Fraud Case

While I had understood the technical details of the product and was impressed by the fact that I was dealing with a super-sharp young mind that was open to possibilities, what was left unanswered for me was the need for Fosun to appoint a CEO at this early stage. Bhavik was extremely upfront in telling me that he had been convicted in a case in the US because of which Fosun didn't want him to front-end the operations.

What followed was a tale that spoke of the wrong choices the guy had made, but also of his fortitude. Apparently, Bhavik had started his career with United Airlines as a pilot in the US. While the money was good and he got to see places, eventually the glamour of the 'drivery' job wore off and he wanted to settle down. That led him to start a grocery store along with a partner, Vijay, in the US. I was impressed when he told me that he didn't want to stop learning, and that in the manner of the character Rancho in *3 Idiots*, he would often walk into colleges and attend lectures, not for the degree but for the learnings. At the time, there was one piece of information he figured out that changed his life irrevocably. He found that if you happened to know someone's social security number, you could have his credit card delivered to your address without authentication. He mentioned this to Vijay, who, armed with this newfound information, actually got access to some credit cards.

Bhavik insisted that Vijay's intention was not to cheat, for when he used the credit cards to buy merchandize he ensured that he made all payments on time. It was only a matter of time, however, before the FBI was at their store and hauled up everyone, including Bhavik, who used to live at Vijay's house. Bhavik claimed that since Vijay was married and had a family, Bhavik took the blame upon himself. What followed was a harrowing time, where eventually Bhavik Koladiya, aka Bob Patel, was convicted in the credit card fraud case, incarcerated for identity theft and put under house arrest with an ankle monitor. He was charged with felony on as many as eighteen counts. On the one hand he chose not to employ a lawyer but to defend himself in court, while on the other hand he used the time of the house arrest to teach himself coding. The case continued, and the prosecutors saw that he was quite sharp. Eventually, he was made an offer, which, if he agreed to it, would lead to the sixteen charges against him being dropped. What he needed for that was to agree to the two least incriminating charges, and also to leave the US and never return. His options, clearly, were to either stay back and fight a long, hard battle or agree to their terms. He chose the latter. 'Back in India, my aim is to do something worthwhile to redeem myself,' he explained to me with a lot of conviction, something that I credited him for.

Bhavik had earlier run a company called BookMyHaircut. It was in solving the payment issues in this venture that he started to look at UPI as an option, and then, of course, one thing led to another, including his running into Fosun. When Fosun got to know of his past, interested as they were in the product, they refused to fund the company with him at the helm. That explained why they were now looking for a CEO. While that was acceptable to Bhavik, what he didn't quite like was the pace at which things were moving at Fosun.

The big picture was clear to me in the first meeting itself. In fact, in many ways, this meeting was like the coming together of co-founders. I realized that the UPI space would be a good problem to solve and that if payments were made free, the data so collected could be used to offer loans and launch digital financial products for merchants.

I told Bhavik and Shashvat that we would need to restructure the company. While we could go with a fair 33 per cent each, despite my years of experience, I felt that Shashvat was very young and didn't bring that much to the table and that it would be good for the two of them to devise a split of the 66 per cent equity among themselves. The 66 per cent was finally split as 42 per cent and 24 per cent between Bhavik and Shashvat, while I went with the balance 34 per cent. The shareholding pattern agreed to, I bought commensurate shares from Bhavik and Shashvat. It was now time to start work on our pitches. Around this time, I was working from a coworking place in a basement in Panchshila Park. I went on to take additional space for the five of them and advised them to work from there. My view was simple: this work had to be done on ground and not from the glass offices of Fosun in DLF Horizon.

Fosun, of course, was the first entity that we pitched to. As against their initial discussion of $250,000, my ask was that we needed to raise $2 million at a $6 million pre-money valuation. To say that Vipin and Tej Kapoor were livid would be an understatement. They took Bhavik to an adjoining room and started venting out on him. They even threatened him with his case and warned him that no one else would give him any money and that his association with me, too, was because of Fosun. Simply put, they were shocked that Bhavik and Shashvat had decided to move out of their fold. While it became fairly clear to

Bhavik that money from Fosun would not be forthcoming, I told them that they could entrust the fundraising to me.

Angel Investors

Thus began the process of my reaching out to my network, convinced in the belief that the product we were setting out to launch would soon be bigger than Paytm, PhonePe, Pine Labs or any of the existing merchant-facing players. My first port of call was Sanjay Rishi of AmEx. I took Bhavik along to Sanjay's house and took him through the details. He agreed to invest Rs 25 lakh and became our first angel investor. Another early investment was that of Akshay Munjal, who came from the eminent Munjal–Hero Group family. I had earlier helped Akshay—whose daughter goes to school with my daughter—with his family office investments. He agreed to commit another Rs 25 lakh. Some of the other early investors included Kunal Khattar, Anshoo Sharma of Magicpin, Nitin Gupta of PayU, AngelList, Venture Catalysts, Navneet Singh of Gram Factory and more. In all, I ended up raising a total of Rs 1.92 crore at a Rs 18-crore pre-money valuation.

Two of the early investors that I approached, but who for some or the other reason couldn't come on board, were Kunal Shah and Jitendra Gupta. Kunal was busy building Cred, the credit card bill payments and rewards platform, and was incommunicado. Jitendra Gupta, who was whiling away his final days at PayU then, was willing to commit Rs 1 crore at an even further discounted Rs 12-crore valuation. But he had to get an approval from PayU for non-conflict. That approval didn't come and, therefore, neither did his funding. I, however, later invited Jitendra to the BharatPe board. Incidentally, Fosun ended up not putting any money into the venture. Vipin's unreasonable and unacceptable ask to Bhavik was that we should give them personal equity in the business as they had put in work in the early days.

It didn't sound right to us, and we decided not to pander to this demand and proceeded without Fosun's participation.

Kala Jaadu

If I thought that having been a part of so many fundraising conversations had prepared me for everything, I was living in a fool's paradise. For nothing could have prepared me for this one phone call.

> '*Tumne hamare bachchon par kala jaadu kar diya hai* (You have done black magic on our kids),' said the voice at the other end.

The last thing that I ever thought I could be accused of was doing black magic. Yet, those were the exact words that I was being blasted with that morning. The 'kids' under question were the 3 IITian wingmates of Shashvat—Tanmay, Yogi and Satyam— who had by now decided to drop out of IIT, midcourse, to pursue their entrepreneurial dreams. Their parents were worried that their children had got carried away and believed that I was the one responsible for this.

It is only later, once the hyper-growth story of BharatPe began, that they realized that we were on to something big. The first BharatPe QR was put out on 15 August 2018, and we never had to look back.

8

The Building Blocks

One QR and Two Legal Notices

Our entry into the world of QR codes was greeted by two legal notices! Since we were offering a QR code with interoperability, it was important that our code had the logos of consumer apps like Paytm, PhonePe and Google Pay, among others. This was what Paytm and PhonePe objected to. I had to dig out the relevant clauses of the trademark law that allowed for fair use of another's trademark, as long as it was for educational purposes and helped in consumer awareness. Paytm, the saner competition, understood this immediately and withdrew. PhonePe, however, wouldn't budge. The legal journey with PhonePe, in fact, transcended this notice and escalated into a clash around the name of the brand BharatPe as well. The case that ran for over two years became the proverbial conversation-opener for every single VC pitch that I entered into subsequently. PhonePe even came after us when we launched PostPe some three years later—my guess is that Sameer Nigam, the founder of PhonePe, genuinely believes that he owns 'Pe' as a suffix.

At the core, PhonePe's problem was that BharatPe was a smart name. Apparently, when the government had introduced BHIM UPI, one of the early names that they had contended with was BharatPe. Bhavik had come across the name in the initial UPI docs, and went ahead and registered the name. Besides being a catchy name with a high recall, the 'Bharat' in our name also inspired trust, as most merchants thought we were a government service, especially because we were free. That, in fact, was PhonePe's primary issue with us.

PhonePe's initial objection was that our logo ('Pe' written in the Devanagari script against a tricolour background) was similar to theirs. We went ahead and changed our logo. Not satisfied, they filed a case against us, stating that we couldn't use the word 'Pe' as it was a distinctive part of their name and our use of the term was an infringement. We defended the case in high court. The answer to 'Whose Pe is it? PhonePe or BharatPe?'—a headline carried by the *Hindu BusinessLine*—came by way of a Bombay High Court ruling noting that PhonePe had no registration of or exclusive right over the word 'Pe', which is widely used in place of 'Pay', and thus there was no case of a copyright infringement. This settled the case, having run its course for over two years amid extensive media coverage.

Early Tech Solution

In the early days we ran with a tech solution that could at best be termed a 'jugaad'. The merchant acquisition journey had begun with 1000 merchants based out of Nehru Place, a sprawling market for computers and computer parts in Delhi. Their QR codes were, in fact, created on the BHIM UPI app to test our thesis. Bhavik's phone number was fed as an additional number for notifications into the BHIM UPI app, so that through his SMSes we would be notified of any transactions. We hadn't, however, budgeted for instances such as if Bhavik was on a flight, we wouldn't receive any notifications for those hours!

I soon realized that, going forward, this arrangement would not work. At the same time, we weren't in the money flow. What we needed was a tie-up with a bank so that when a customer made a transaction, that money could come into our bank account, and, in turn, we could then settle the merchant account in real time.

The first bank that I opened up a relationship with was Yes Bank, having done a lot of work with them while I was at Grofers. While we had made the transaction free for the merchant, we had to pay the bank both on the incoming (0.65 per cent on transactions above Rs 2000) and outgoing transactions. Our pitch to the bank, therefore, was that we were incurring our own merchant acquisition to scale the business and in the process increasing the free float for the bank. The first, critical banking partnership in place, I asked Bhavik to have his engineers stationed at Yes Bank's Mumbai office and get the whole thing executed seamlessly. We had at the outset set aside ESOPs for the three IITians who had joined along with Shashvat. Additionally, we hired an external tech agency and also hired final-year students from Shashvat's dad's engineering college, keeping our tech costs under strict check.

I then pressed ahead with the next critical piece: real-time onboarding of merchants. The earlier model was that of acquiring a merchant and taking their bank account details, and then sending them a joining kit with their specific QR codes. This involved critical lead time. I ensured that we created pre-printed QR kits that led to instant onboarding of merchants. All that was required to be done was to enter the merchant's bank account number and IFSC code, and the QR code would be linked at the merchant's premises itself. Importantly, our proposition that we wouldn't charge the merchant any fee and would settle payments in real time was a big plus, as merchants in those days were used to dealing with Paytm and PhonePe, that not only deducted a 2 per cent fee on every transaction but also settled their accounts on a T+2 basis, i.e. two full days after the transaction was done.

While Bhavik began to look after the tech piece, I had my hands full with managing strategy, banking relationships, new product launches, fundraising as well as team-building. We therefore asked Shashvat to focus on distribution and launch the product in different cities.

An Employee Number before Mine

Once the number of transactions grew, the other aspect that needed close supervision was the admin piece. While it was easy to recruit someone for the role, we had to keep our costs under check. The one name that instantly struck me was Madhuri. Having run her own business for a while, she was great at handling management, admin and managing people in general. However, it would only be fair that the other co-founders approved of her joining. 'You must bring her in. Knowing that we have someone trustworthy looking at things internally, we can scale,' was the unanimous reaction of both Bhavik and Shashvat. Till this time, since I hadn't been formally relieved from PCJ, I couldn't become a director in the company. Madhuri, therefore, became the director, with her employee number preceding mine. She was soon initiated to handle leases, vendor management, printer coordination and more. Additionally, since we didn't have any HR team, the added responsibility of the HR function also fell on her. With her in charge of the admin piece and knowing that there was a competent, right-intentioned person, I could look outwards and focus on our growth.

Knocking on VC Doors

With our internal systems in place, it was about time for me to look at additional fundraising. In fact, there wasn't a single VC whose doors I didn't knock on in those days. An extremely interesting early meeting was with Mohit Bhatnagar of Sequoia, where we had to start off by explaining how UPI works in the first place. This was despite the fact that this was an investor who had not just invested in Citrus Pay but had also ensured an exit for them. 'Give me your phone and your debit card,' I told him, certain that till the time the VCs themselves transacted through it they would not understand that UPI is the future. I then created an account for him on the PhonePe app, linking it to his HSBC card. A peer-to-peer transaction done, he was quite taken by the magic of UPI. However, despite his initial excitement, for the next three months Sequoia didn't put any money on us. The primary reason for this was that Sequoia owned more than 70 per cent stake in Pine Labs. They realized that with our entry, Pine Labs would lose its market share. They therefore wanted to give time to Pine Labs to develop this technology. By that time, Lokvir, the original founder of Pine Labs, had moved on, and Pine Labs was more of an infrastructure as opposed to a tech company. It was only when Pine Labs couldn't develop the technology that Sequoia decided to invest in us. Not without a big FOMO nudge from Beenext, technically the first VC that identified our potential!

Teru San

'Come to Singapore.' Those were Teru San's parting words as we ended our one-hour-long call. I was introduced to him and his company Beenext by one of my angel investors, Navneet Singh of PepperTap, who was also my batchmate from IIM Ahmedabad. Teru San had realized on the initial call itself that we were trying to solve a big problem by offering interoperability. My immediate concern, however, was that travelling to Singapore meant spending money, which I was trying hard to control, given that so far we had only raised Rs 1.92 crore from angel investors. I, however, decided to take this chance and make a day trip to Singapore, so that I didn't have to spend any additional money on a hotel stay.

Having landed at Changi Airport, I headed straight to the Beenext office. I had carried one of our preprinted kits, and did a quick demo of onboarding Teru San as a merchant and conducting some dummy transactions. Teru San was a quintessential Japanese gentleman who wasn't too emotionally expressive, and it was hard to fathom if he liked what he saw. I had placed my ask of $2 million at a $6 million pre-money value, but all I heard from Teru San was a cryptic 'Let's go for lunch'. I was rather disheartened that my trip had come to nothing, although I tried not to show it during the short walk to a Vietnamese joint for lunch, accompanied by Teru San and one of his colleagues, a gentleman called Nao.

The conversation at lunch revolved around the fintech space, our families and more, with no mention of any proposed funding. It was only on the way back from lunch that Teru San expressed his desire to invest $750,000. I was over the moon. So far, all institutional investors that I had met had been dismissive of our ability to fight giants such as the SoftBank- and Alibaba-funded Paytm; the Walmart-backed PhonePe; Google Pay; and the imminent, Facebook-backed WhatsApp Pay. Not many investors globally had the gall to put money against the top five cash-generating tech giants who owned the UPI space. This was the first win from a VC and a big validation.

The euphoria lasted till the time I reached the airport, when my phone rang and Teru San's number flashed on it. In the few seconds before I picked up his call, I was convinced that Teru San had changed his mind. 'Ashneer San, can I ask you something?' he began while my heart thumped. 'Can I increase the investment to $1 million?' went his request. I couldn't have been more relieved as I immediately agreed to his proposal. I was in a daze throughout the flight back to India. We were certainly on the brink of something big. Only as I switched on my phone on landing, Teru San's name flashed yet again and so did my fears. I was certain that Teru San had used the hours while I was suspended thousands of feet high in the air to do some due diligence and didn't have good tidings to share. This time around, I was even more surprised. 'Can I increase the investment to $1.5 million, Ashneer San?' was his query. While I thanked him profusely for the trust he was reposing in us, I had to tell him that since I was looking at raising a total of $2 million, if he invested as much as $1.5 million, there would be nothing left for the second investor. He understood my concern and agreed to keep his investment at $1 million. True to his word, he not only signed the term sheet but also wired the $1 million to us by the end of the month.

When I received the term sheet from Teru San and shared the news with Sequoia, they finally woke up and started thinking of investing in us with some seriousness. While Teru San was extremely proactive in his decision-making, getting Sequoia on board was quite a Herculean task. Little did I know that there was more drama in store.

Skeleton in the Closet

'We can't go ahead with the investment.'

I was shocked to get a phone call from Harshjit Sethi of Sequoia, the principal who was leading the investment in us, one morning. This was after we had gone through the due diligence and the necessary documentation. On my inquiring what had changed, he said that they had found out that Bhavik had been convicted in a credit card fraud case in the US. They were upset with me that, being privy to this information, I hadn't shared it with them. My point of view was extremely simple. It wasn't for me to share details of Bhavik's past, especially as I wasn't sitting in judgement over him. In fact, to me and to my angel investors, it wasn't an issue at all. As a co-founder, it clearly was Bhavik's prerogative to share this information (or not). Harshjit, however, wasn't convinced and wanted us to take the matter up with his CFO and general counsel. I asked Bhavik to go to Bangalore and meet them to explain his case. Clearly, they had to be comfortable with his explanation, as opposed to me selling his case.

In the meantime, Sequoia also called Teru San to tell him of this development. Fortunately for us, we hadn't touched the money received from Teru San and it was still lying in the capital account. I assured Teru San that if he wanted to withdraw, I would wire the money to him instantly and that he shouldn't feel that his money was stuck. Teru San, however, wasn't worried.

Bhavik's meeting at Sequoia didn't yield the necessary result, as Sequoia's final decision was that in order for them to put money into our venture, Bhavik needed to be off the cap table. Their view was that it was necessary to attract future capital and get licences from the regulators. It clearly wasn't my call. I made it clear to Sequoia that if this was their decision, they would need to convey it to Bhavik. As far as I was concerned, if Bhavik didn't want to exit, I would stand by him. I was also clear that the implication of this decision was that I would have to return Rs 1.92 crore to my angel investors. My backup plan, in that case, was to sell my Malviya Nagar house to repay them. While, eventually, all my angel investors earned between 80–250x cash returns on their initial investment, I reminded them on their exits that their investment had been totally risk-free from the very beginning, as there was no way I would let them down.

Sequoia referred me back to Harshal Kamdar of PwC to arrive at a structure whereby Bhavik's shares could be bought over. Harshal had earlier helped me with the Grofers externalization, and I knew him well. The option presented was that Bhavik's shares could be bought over by multiple people for a lumpsum amount of Rs 4 crore. I, however, left the decision entirely to Bhavik.

Bhavik decided to go with Sequoia's offer, and his shares were picked up by Beenext, Sequoia and the coming in of some angels, including Shashvat's dad, Shashvat and me. Not only was Bhavik's name taken off the shareholders' agreement, he also resigned from the board and ceased to be on the rolls of the company, working as an external consultant instead. For me, personally, he continued to hold the status of initial partner, even though he had no locus standi as one, in the official scheme of things. He also sat in on all board meetings as an observer. In fact, even today, I feel sad about his exit at such an early stage at Sequoia's behest.

The issue resolved, we were awaiting the committed funding to come from Sequoia as well as for Teru San's formal tick-off to use his $1 million. As far as the angel round of Rs 1.92 crore was concerned, the money was nearly consumed. I was now staring at a situation where the employee salary payout for the Diwali month was to happen, and we had no money in our official account. I knew that I had to hold the fort till we had the funds in place. I therefore asked Madhuri to transfer the salary bill amount from her personal account to the BharatPe account for us to get through the month of November 2018. Hopefully, we thought, by the time we hit next month, the funds would have arrived in our bank account. Therefore, we felt more relief than elation on the completion of $2 million seed round at a pre-money valuation of $5 million and a post-money valuation of $7 million.

Once we had our funding in place, Madhuri resigned as the director of the company and I came on the board, although she continued to play an important role as an employee. With Bhavik getting off the cap table, I didn't want the other co-founder to ever feel that I was trying to be in control of the board, even though I had an option of having another founder nominee on the board. In fact, with Madhuri's exit, Sequoia got a board seat. In hindsight, though, this turned out to be a big mistake, as this was the time I should have inducted Madhuri as a co-founder. One of the many lessons that I have learnt in my entrepreneurial journey is that if you do not position a capable person correctly at the right time, it becomes a big constraint.

On the business front we continued to grow, and by December of the same year I had to inform Sequoia and Beenext that I was looking at raising an additional $10 million. On a phone call, they asked me not to reach out to new investors and said that they would be interested in participating in the round. The December round saw Beenext and Sequoia participate for $2 million and $8 million respectively, at a $30 million pre-money valuation. I had no idea that I was soon to have a surprise investor.

Around that time I got introduced to a young, spunky American Sardarji called Vinny Pujji, who was the senior investment associate at Insight Partners. He happened to be a distant relative of my cousin and was visiting India at the time from the US. In fact, my meeting with Vinny Pujji was scheduled for the same day as I signed the term sheet with Sequoia. It took Vinny only that one meeting to confirm that he wanted to put in the dollars. 'The round is now closed. Besides, I do not want to dilute any more equity,' I apologetically informed Vinny. 'I will pay a premium. I don't have the patience to wait for the next round,' was his instant response, and I was taken aback by it. In a big validation for the business we were building, Insight Partners paid a 25 per cent premium on the same day the Sequoia term sheet was signed. To date, Insight Partners is one of the major shareholders in BharatPe, and BharatPe continues to be one of their biggest holdings in India. All of this was made possible on account of the maturity and prudence of this lanky Sardar,

Vinny Pujji, who was not even thirty yet. Vinny later left Insight Partners to form a VC fund which raised over US$1 billion, Left Lane Partners, in which I am a proud LP (limited partner).

Death Forecast

'I think you will die.' While I had just received a huge validation from Vinny, another investor made a forecast that my business would die. This was Meyer 'Micky' Malka, of Ribbit Capital. Micky is considered to be the big fish in the fintech world, globally. If he puts money into any start-up, every other fund tends to derive a validation. Yet here was Micky telling me that my business wouldn't survive. 'If you know that BharatPe will die, can you also predict the date of death?' I asked him, albeit a bit cheekily. 'Two months,' he said without an iota of doubt. 'What happens if I do not die in two months?' I persisted. 'Then I will write you a cheque,' came his response. This was one promise I was sure I would hold Micky to.

9

The Stairway to Success

'Take the stairway to success.' That was the seemingly metaphorical message that Madhuri had put in the lift lobby of the building in Malviya Nagar, in which our office was located on the second floor. We had moved into this office in early 2019 by taking half of the available 5000 square feet of space. The very fact that we had shifted into this office, to me, was a sign from above, as its boundary touched the Arya Samaj that my grandfather had founded and served till his last days. In fact, the landlord who was otherwise quite finicky about tenants had agreed to rent the space out to me, only because he had deep respect for my grandfather. In my heart, I knew that this wasn't a coincidence.

Coming back to the message on the lift, with the motivating wordplay, what we were doing was literally asking people to take the stairs. Our primary agenda was to save the cost of operating the lift and make it tough for employees to go down on chai-and-sutta breaks. From the beginning we were clear that we had to keep our costs strictly under check and not go on a splurging spree just because we had money in our bank. The other thing that I kept a stringent check on was the size of the team. I firmly believed that as a tech company, if you had to hire a disproportionately high number of people for business growth, it was a sign of your being an operations-heavy non-tech business. We ran a tight ship, starting with some sixty-odd people on half the floor, which went up to a strength of 125 when we took up the entire floor. Additionally, when we set up a tech office in the next building, we operated with another sixty engineers.

What I continued to work on, in the meantime, were several game-changing products.

Bank, aka Jagannath Ka Rath

Having been a banker for a large part of my life, the one thing I had seen at close range was the fact that a bank works in silos or fiefdoms, with the customer just being incidental to the business. *Bank ek Jagannath ka rath hai; sab employees haath laga kar khade hai, chala kaun raha hai pata nahi.* A bank is a juggernaut; all employees are giving it a hand, but no one knows who is running it.

My inherent dislike for bankers, however, stems from the fact that while every other profession is trying to wow their customers, banks run their business on the principle of intimidating their own customers. If you walk into a branch and ask for a loan, you will be inspected from head to toe and a quick judgement will be passed—*English nahi aati, chappal pehni hai, kaise kapde pehne hai* (you do not speak in English or aren't dressed well) will be just some of the biases of the bank manager that will raise their ugly head. So much for the cliché that the customer is king! Interestingly, if they aren't inclined to give you the loan, you will rarely hear a no directly. In his fancy English, honed at an elite institution, the banker will tell you how the internal risk department has flagged your case or that the auditor doesn't allow it; or, better still, they will pass on the blame to the most common scapegoat, the RBI. I would even go to the extent of saying that *agar saamne se saanp aur banker aa rahe ho, toh banker ko latth mar do*, if you encounter a banker and a snake, hit the banker, the chances of survival are greater that way.

These are the exact attitudes that I set out to change. My philosophy of building BharatPe was that the customer cannot be intimidated and should be treated fairly, on the basis of easy data and without any biases. Now that is something that a tech product that works on an algorithm can do. In fact, the products that I launched at BharatPe, in quick succession, were launched with this objective. My belief is that while banking will always remain a service, fintech being a product works better for customers and is much more scalable. Also, technology being a bank's Achilles' heel, bankers will never be able to learn technology as fast as fintechs will learn finance and business.

Lending Product

As early as April 2019, we launched a lending product based on the purest philosophy of lending—cashflow discounting. Early on, we realized that merchants in India are a harried lot. Not only are their margins poor, while they offer credit to customers, but when it comes to expanding their business, the neighbourhood kirana shop has nearly no borrowing options in the formal sector. *Banks ko dukandar pe credit card machine lagani hai aur current account bechna hai bas—koi lending hai hi nahi.* The only business banks need from shopkeepers is to install a card-acceptance machine and manage the current account; bankers don't lend to shopkeepers. That leaves them very often at the mercy of loan sharks charging 3–4 per cent interest a month. It was to solve this problem that we built a lending product into the app itself, as I wanted to offer it as a product and not a solution.

Since we were in the cashflow of merchants, we knew exactly how much business they were transacting every month; on the basis of that we started lending to merchants at an interest rate of 2 per cent per month. The interesting bit was that in our case, we didn't need to wait to collect our money at the end of the month; instead, we would do so from the amount coming through the merchant QR, daily, in an automated fashion. If through the BharatPe QR, a merchant was accepting payments of Rs 1000 daily, he now had the added ability of getting a loan on the basis of that of Rs 1,00,000, which he could repay over a year, with Rs 400 deducted automatically every day (Sunday being a no-deduction day). For the first time, the shopkeeper was getting a quantum of loan on the basis of his business on the BharatPe QR, and the loan was getting repaid automatically through transactions on the same QR. My philosophy was simple: if you build something fundamental, the market tends to adopt it and the product then has a lifetime value. It is on this principle that we have cumulatively disbursed almost $1 billion, earning an IRR (internal rate of return) of 48 per cent effectively as our collections happen daily.

Within twelve months of launch, I had therefore acquired millions of merchants pan India, made merchant fees (called MDR—Merchant Discount Rate) zero for the industry and was earning 48 per cent IRR on lending, with our collection rates far higher than the players who had been around for decades.

I had, by this time, adopted a mindset of launching a new product every six months and also ensured that we had the right people to hyperscale these products. While I didn't hire any stalwarts from the NBFC or the banking world, I made sure I brought in people who were passionate about the business.

Mahine Ka Ek Taka

I have often been told that my products are too simple. While it may be pointed out as an affront, in fact, this is the very reason for their success. Our merchant investment product is one such. I have never understood why no interest is allowed to be paid on current accounts, other than to give free money to banks to improve their margins. My idea was to offer a current account that enabled merchants to earn a 12 per cent annualized interest on their capital while also offering them liquidity with a single click. My team debated keeping the rate of return low, closer to 7 per cent that banks offered as the best rates for FD, for us to be able to earn more margins. I was, however, extremely clear that we needed to earn the trust of merchants. Besides, I knew that the virality of this product would come in part from the fact that at 1 per cent a month, the math was easy to do. I would give credit for this in part to Madhuri's Baniya business family that spoke in simple business terms. '*Mahine ka ek taka*'—1 per cent a month—I knew from their experience, was a good number for excess liquidity. Also, a high rate ensures stickiness—despite its being an instantly liquid product with no lock-in, I never saw deposits degrow.

Later, of course, when we needed even more capital to lend, we also made a foray into the consumer space—with my favourite product, 12% Club. It is the only financial product in the world where the lending rate and the borrowing rate for customers are the same—12 per cent. Also, it is the only financial product where the liability generated is more than the loans given out at 12 per cent, the excess amount being given to our merchants, earning BharatPe an IRR of 48 per cent.

All the while I was very clear that this game couldn't be won so much by capital as through innovation and seamless execution on the ground.

Micky's Promise

One summer evening, sometime in May 2019, I received a phone call with three powerful words: 'Let's do this.' The caller, Micky

Malka, had noticed that we had not only 'not died' in the prior months but that our numbers were on the increase. He was now ready to act on his promise of writing us a cheque.

What followed was a fundraising trip to the US to meet several investors, including Micky. Having travelled economy for fourteen long hours, I landed in San Francisco. I was clear that I didn't want to spend any money staying in hotels and on $100 Uber trips. I therefore rented a car, to cover a journey of about an hour and a half to my sister-in-law's place in Sacramento. Having flown in on a weekend, I was in for some marathon meetings, beginning the following Monday. Since I had even sent my seed round deck to SoftBank, there was no way I wanted to miss meeting any investors for this round. While some may think that it was an oversell of sorts, the fact remains that you cannot hesitate to go out there and tell your story. Today, while I have built a strong reputation for my fundraising abilities, what people often fail to see is the sheer hard work that goes into these pitches. One needs to pitch to 100 investors at least three times to get ten of them to commit.

As luck would have it, the day before I had to meet Micky at the Ribbit office, my meetings stretched late into the evening. A drive to Sacramento at that hour was nearly impossible. I was left with no option but to book a hotel and stay the night in Palo Alto to be able to make it to the Ribbit meeting on time the next morning. Only I wasn't carrying a change of clothes. That meant sleeping in the same set of clothes, taking a shower and getting to the Ribbit office hoping that the clothes didn't look slept-in. The only luxury I had was to walk up to a pharmacy and buy a pack of combs to have my hair in place before entering their office above the famous Apple Store at University Avenue. So much for the glamour that is associated with fundraising! Incidentally, slept-in clothes notwithstanding, Micky lived up to his commitment. I managed to close the $50-million Series B, led by Ribbit Capital along with Steadview.

Salman Khan

Around this time, I was approached by someone unconventional—Bollywood megastar Salman Khan's manager. Turns out, Salman's film *Bharat* was releasing in June that year, chronicling the eponymous journey of the transition of a man and a nation. He felt that there was an opportunity for BharatPe to collaborate, as it seemed to be a good fit. Even though BharatPe wasn't really a consumer-facing brand, I knew that I had to undertake the brand-building exercise sooner rather than later. This tie-up would be a bold call also on account of the fact that Salman Khan had been controversy's favourite child, and brands were still hesitant to join hands with him for fear of negative publicity. I decided to go ahead and enter into a conversation on the endorsement fee, which began at Rs 7.5 crore and which was finally negotiated down to Rs 4.25 crore.

With Series B underway, I had less than Rs 100 crore in the bank at the time, of which I was committing Rs 15 crore to the Salman-led campaign. Early June was when we shot the ad, directed by a new small company called Fat Men. The ad turned out to be quite peppy and popular, and the first one in the country targeted at small shopkeepers. I spent three hours with Salman prior to the shoot and found him to be absolutely worldly-wise as against the popular perception. Our QRs now had Salman Khan's picture on them, endorsing our offerings. In fact, it was BharatPe's successful association with Salman Khan that later forced PhonePe to look at celebrity endorsements with Aamir Khan and Alia Bhatt, as they thought we now had an added advantage.

Hunt for a Chief Business Officer

With the business expanding and with my hands full, I realized that we needed someone to execute daily operations so that strategic growth wasn't stemmed. I gave a mandate to look for a chief business officer. A headhunter sent us the CV of one Suhail Sameer, which I found quite interesting. Having started his career as one of the youngest associate partners at McKinsey, he, at the time, worked at the RP–Sanjiv Goenka Group. I invited him home for dinner to be able to understand him and his work motivations better. On meeting him, I quite liked the guy and found him to be driven. Sharing his family history, he told me that his dad was a Kashmiri Pandit, while his mom was a Muslim, and that since his dad worked for SBI International, he had lived overseas in his growing-up years. Having studied at the Delhi College of Engineering and then at IIM Lucknow, he had joined McKinsey, where he majorly handled the energy sector. This was where he happened to meet Sanjiv Goenka and eventually joined him at the conglomerate level. What also caught my interest was that Suhail claimed that he had launched their snacking brand, Too Yum, and had taken it to a turnover of Rs 500 crore.

'Sanjiv Goenka's son is now about to join the business, and I do not want to build for an heir apparent to take over.' This was his reply when I asked him why he was considering a move. Our conversation continued over dinner as I offered him a drink from my dad's fully stocked bar, apologizing for the fact that I couldn't join him as I didn't drink myself. When it came to discussing his salary expectations, though, there was a disconnect. Suhail mentioned that while he was drawing a salary of around Rs 6 crore, there was a Rs 15-crore payout that was due to him from his company, which he wanted me to make good, if he were to join. Since that wasn't a number I was looking at, that conversation died there.

The team otherwise, of course, continued to go from strength to strength. To make sure that they felt comfortable as we took on a high-growth trajectory, I offered my house, which had been lying empty, for them to stay at. Bhavik lived in my fully furnished Malviya Nagar house for over two years, and I didn't charge him any rent as I felt that we were partners in growth. In fact, even my parents' house in Malviya Nagar was occupied by ten-odd early-career engineers who would've otherwise struggled to get a place on rent for such a large group. Bhavik and Shashvat had harboured this juvenile desire to one day move back to Gujarat. While I explained to them that no unicorn so far had come from Gujarat, I also went out of my way to make them more comfortable in Delhi.

Ending the Year on a High Note

The year 2019 ended with yet another hectic fundraising trip to the US. This time I was accompanied by a guy called Aviral Gupta, who had joined us earlier that year. He had interned with me in Grofers and thereafter had gone to the London Business School. Having returned to India, though, he couldn't find a relevant assignment. When he approached me for a job, I made an offer to him to work with me on fundraising. The one memory I have of Aviral from that trip is his being thoroughly exhausted and sleeping between meetings as I drove for miles from one hectic meeting to another, mentally preparing for the next pitch. Clearly, it was the mission at hand that gave me that added boost of adrenalin—I was tiring much younger folks out with my sheer relentlessness. And sure enough, it paid off. This time we ended the round with raising $75 million in Series C funding, led by Coatue Management at a $425 million post-money valuation.

Clearly, 2019 had turned out to be one hell of a year, with literally three funding rounds, two major product launches, a big campaign launch and, importantly, a valuation of nearly half a billion dollars. There was literally no other start-up in India that had gone from $0 to $425 million valuation in as few as fifteen months at that time.

10

Souring Relationships

'Keep It at Thirty-Six Lakh'

In keeping company costs under check, the one place where I did not make any exception was to keep my own salary low. After months of unrelenting work and delivering growth, and having drawn next to nothing as salary, I wrote to Harshjit Singh at Sequoia, wanting to increase my own salary. To my proposal of increasing my salary to Rs 60 lakh per annum, I was advised to keep it at Rs 36 lakh. It was the first reality check for me that while VCs draw millions of dollars as salaries themselves, they are loath to see founders get their due. It's absolutely perverse logic, which is driven by their own false belief that money does all the hard work and they can, therefore, treat founders as unpaid slaves.

What I did have from Sequoia, along with the closure of Series C in January 2020, was a written commitment on email to buy founder and ESOP shares in secondary of $3 million, of which $1 million were to come from Beenext and $2 million from Sequoia.

'I have an investment committee meeting on Monday, and I will have the secondary approved—it's just a formality,' Harshjit promised me over a weekend. I waited until Wednesday to call Harshjit. I knew something was wrong the moment he started to speak to me in formal English. 'There has been some issue with our investment structure, because of which we cannot commit more capital from our existing fund,' was the vague, unconvincing excuse thrown at me. Clearly, I was being lied to— something that I don't take lightly. After all, it was on Harshjit's commitment on behalf of Sequoia that Teru San had bought $1 million of secondary. What bothered me besides the fact that they were going back on their commitment, was that in a round of $75 million, in which Harshjit had me push all the incoming investors on the valuation ask, Sequoia did not feel the need to participate even optically. I would rather be told that despite all my hard work his seniors hadn't agreed to the secondary, or even that they had found the proposition risky. To be dishonest and to pass the buck to some restructuring operation, in true banker style, was demeaning to my intelligence. In hindsight, I lost faith in Harshjit and Sequoia that day. Not only did I stop taking his calls, I also told Bhavik, who was getting married around the time and for whose wedding we were all flying to Bhavnagar, that he shouldn't expect me to engage with Harshjit during the wedding. This episode was clearly an early sign of their malicious intent.

Yes Bank Ltd Placed under Moratorium

Not deterred by this event, I was in Pune for a rather audacious task in March 2020. We needed someone experienced and driven to lead our lending operations, and I had decided to interview the most touted senior team at Bajaj Finance. Not only did this team have years of experience, they were also drawing crores in salaries and ESOPs, and had an amazing lifestyle in tony Pune. I was totally prepared that one of them would turn around and tell me, '*Bhai, charas pee ke aaya hai kya* (Are you doped)?' With my experience, however, I had learnt that it was important to aim big. Interestingly, the entire team interviewed with me—either out of intrigue or perhaps to find out their own market value. It was amid this daring personal move that I was hit with a big piece of news—that as of 5 March 2020, Yes Bank was placed under a thirty-day moratorium.

The financial position of Yes Bank had, of course, been going downhill for a while, but this was unexpected. At BharatPe, Yes Bank was our partner acquiring bank—most of our cash-in and cash-out happened through Yes Bank current accounts, as our QR codes had Yes Bank UPI handles. Lately, we had also tied up with ICICI Bank. Our current standing was that while 70 per cent of our business was still on Yes Bank QR codes, 30 per cent of our transactions were happening through ICICI QR codes. With the Yes Bank accounts being frozen, 70 per cent of our QRs had stopped working overnight.

Bhavik, who had gone for his honeymoon to New Zealand, happened to land in India on the very day amid this debacle. Our challenge was that it was impossible to physically change all the QRs; we therefore needed a tech solution, whereby ICICI Bank QRs could run through the same handles. Bhavik took up the task along with his team, and within twenty-four hours everything was mapped in the back-end, from Yes Bank's handle to that of ICICI Bank. The PhonePe guys did the same and also came live in twenty-four hours; of course, they were in a bigger soup, as 100 per cent of their operations, both on the merchant and consumer side, were through Yes Bank.

In yet another audacious move, I took this opportunity to write to the Walmart board stating that as the competitor of their investee PhonePe, we had exhibited far more insight in de-risking our business than PhonePe and were taking market share away from them every day. I also went on to make an offer to them, for them to sell the merchant side of the PhonePe business to

BharatPe, while offering them a non-compete that we wouldn't make the foray to the consumer side. While it may sound like a brazen act, the fact remains that the best time to make an offer to a competitor is when they are in distress or doubt. If they would've taken my offer, they wouldn't have had to compete today with strong products such as 12% Club, PostPe and Unity SFB. In fact, PhonePe, to date, has not lent a single penny to any merchant.

NBFC Licence

Having come out of the Yes Bank crisis, we were hit with yet another setback in March 2020. So far, for our lending piece we had been working with NBFC partners such as LiquiLoans, LenDenClub, Hindon and Mamta Projects. While we had taken a timely minority equity in Mamta Projects and Hindon as a company, I had strategically invested in LenDenClub and LiquiLoans. Along the way, however, it was getting clear to me that we needed to have a lending licence of our own. Not being regulated was never a real long-term option. The choice really was between wanting to be regulated as a payment aggregator or a lender. Since at its core our business was that of lending, I was clear that we should have a lending licence.

As early as August 2019, therefore, I had started the application process for an NBFC licence and had set up a subsidiary company by the name of Resilient Capital Private Limited. In March 2020, however, we received a letter from the RBI that our NBFC application had been returned (not rejected). This was because the RBI was unable to do due diligence on investors based out of Mauritius, with Mauritius having been put in February 2020 on the Financial Action Task Force's 'grey list'. Incidentally, the Mauritius investor, on account of which our application was returned, was Sequoia. This was a definite setback for us and perhaps the second nail in our relationship with Sequoia.

Not one to be deterred, I resolved to overcome this issue. I even went out and made the bold promise to the investors that while our NBFC application had been returned, I would now get a banking licence. But at this stage I had little idea how. Of course, later I went on to become the only founder in the whole of the Indian fintech ecosystem to have fulfilled that promise!

The spate of crisis management operations continued that year until the entire country hit the stop button with the announcement of a nationwide lockdown at the end of March 2020. Ever since the launch of BharatPe, we had delivered month-on-month growth. For the first time since August 2018, April 2020 turned out to be an outlier. For us, the problem was exaggerated, as not only was the whole nation on hold but the government had also offered a moratorium on loans. Our saving grace, however, was that our old book wasn't too big, given the fact that we only had one year of lending operations behind us.

To our good fortune, UPI as a mode of payment began to witness huge growth as soon as the markets opened up, as people were wary of exchanging virus-carrying currency notes. For six months, from September 2019 to March 2020, UPI transactions that had flattened out at 1.2 billion transactions a month, further dipped to 0.9 billion transactions in April 2020. But within a year of lockdown, UPI transactions jumped 3x, to a whopping 3.6 billion transactions a month. With many people travelling back to their hometowns during the COVID wave, UPI also made a foray into tier-2 and -3 towns. Clearly, the nationwide lockdown gave a big boost to UPI as a payment methodology.

Given this scenario, and the fact that we were the only lending player with a direct view of business on the ground, we could now also resume our lending operations. Most other players wouldn't resume their lending operations until the end of the year, and this gave us a definite advantage.

Suhail Sameer

The incessant growth meant that there was an immediate need for someone who could handle day-to-day operations. I happened to, out of the blue, call Suhail Sameer, whom I had met for a chief business officer position. At the time, though, he had been waiting for Rs 15 crore from the Goenka group, which I would have never bought out.

I called him to the office, and the sight of the man that greeted me was very unlike the person I had met before. Having lost a lot of weight, he looked like a fraction of his previous self; he now sported a long 'Maulana' beard, which had also totally transformed his look. '*Vella baitha hoon* (I am sitting idle),' he confessed when I asked him what he was doing these days. Apparently, on receiving his Rs 15 crore (never verified) from the RP–Sanjiv Goenka Group, he had quit the organization and was now looking for a new assignment. As our conversation progressed, I made him an offer of Rs 1.75 crore as fixed salary along with handsome ESOPs. I also designated him as the group president. My idea was simple: while I was solving the larger problem, I needed someone to execute it efficiently. I positioned him in a manner that all CXOs would report to him from a business-execution standpoint and to me from a larger strategic, product and people perspective.

Around the same time, I made another hire, that of a CHRO, Jasneet Kaur, who was to report to me since I was responsible for people's growth. These two appointments would turn out to be two of the four biggest hiring mistakes of my career.

In the coming months, I found Suhail scoring high from the work-ethic standpoint. I would see him come to work early in the morning and spend long hours. He was also obviously spending time and energy making friends with people in the organization, for I saw several people hopeful of the CEO position themselves, who had been apprehensive about his joining, coming around.

While he was a great administrator, my only challenge was that he couldn't really look at the bigger picture or present any original ideas. In terms of execution, though, I didn't have any complaints.

However, a small incident around that time had me surprised. I received a phone call from Dhruv Dhanraj Bahl, the chief operating officer at BharatPe, who was also additionally looking at the people function until Jasneet joined as CHRO. He informed me that he had received an anonymous email about a lady we were looking to hire as Suhail's EA. That morning, though, Dhruv received a mail from someone saying that we were making a big mistake as Suhail had an affair with this lady and that she was one of the reasons he was asked to leave the RP–Sanjiv Goenka Group.

While I was shocked to hear the bit about his being asked to leave, my natural instinct is to give people the benefit of the doubt. I could either probe the matter in detail now or simply not hire this lady. I chose the latter option. I remember calling Suhail to tell him that this was what we had learnt, and that we weren't going ahead and hiring the lady in question. Suhail laughed the matter off and said that it was fine if we didn't hire her. While this matter ended there, several other events that transpired over a period of time made me realize that I should have been far more careful in this rather crucial appointment and also taken feedback from his ex-colleagues directly.

Twitter Campaign

While I had my hands full with a number of strategic and operational issues, sometime in the summer of 2020, I woke up to a series of tweets by the CEO of Pine Labs, Amrish Rau. The tweets clearly targeted BharatPe without naming the company. Rau's apparent grouse on Twitter was that some 'small' fintech companies were destroying the Indian payments ecosystem with their 0 per cent MDR offerings. I decided to WhatsApp Rau to ask him why he was putting out these tweets. His reply, that we were spoiling the market and that there were people in the ministry who shared his views, irked me. '*Ministry ki dhamki kise de rahe ho* (Who are you threatening with the ministry)?' I asked. He replied that I should know better, and it was a veiled threat that I didn't take to kindly.

Sequoia held a 70 per cent stake in Pine Labs, and Amrish was known to be very close to Shailendra Singh, the MD of Sequoia, with both of them based out of Singapore. Pine Labs was Shailendra's investment—and therefore high up on their priority list, irrespective of merit. In fact, Sequoia had mandated to give Amrish a $50-million personal outcome on taking Pine Labs public at a $3-billion-plus valuation. It is another matter that over time, with the rise of UPI, Pine Labs turned out to be one of the biggest losers, with card transactions stagnating and credit also getting added to the UPI rails. I wrote to Sequoia in unequivocal terms that they should call off the dogs. This peeved Shailendra, who, in turn, called Micky Malka, to tell him that I was becoming too big for my boots. Micky, while agreeing with Sequoia's political character, counselled me that I shouldn't have written to Sequoia and said that they could very well dump my stock. I explained to Micky that I was minding my own business all along and had only retaliated when I was targeted. However, respecting Micky, I agreed to apologize.

Jitendra Gupta of PayU, who was on my board, offered to intervene, and I got on a call with Sequoia to render my apology. The relationship with Sequoia, however, had gone too far south— they even took the decision to strike my name off as a speaker at their virtual Pit Stop event, their annual investor conference, held in August 2020.

Around the time this entire episode was unfolding, Micky put on the table his added worry that we could be losing the regulatory game. His overhang of regulation, in fact, came from the fact that Ribbit had invested in a fintech called Robinhood in the US and had suffered greatly. Named after the legendary medieval outlaw who took from the rich and gave to the poor, Robinhood had set out to democratize finance, but things didn't quite turn out that way. The company had been stifled for months when the Fed had come down heavily on them for taking consumer deposits.

In our case, while our NBFC licence hadn't come through, there were enough and more people who would poke the RBI on our innovative and successful P2P investing business. While some of the competitors couldn't innovate on technology to enter the space themselves, others struggled to convince their compliance guys to give them a go-ahead and hence gave in to the crab mentality to pull people down. It was clear that we needed to head towards a banking licence, as our propositions were scaling up rapidly in the market.

I realized that till the time I had a licence in place, I needed a credible banking face to liaison with the RBI and to offer them the right picture of our products, not the story that our competition was selling. It was at this time that I reached out to Kewal Handa to come on our board. His wife's parents and my grandparents were good friends. Kewal had had an illustrious corporate career. As the finance director of Pfizer, he had pulled the plug on many factories manufacturing spurious drugs. So much so that the mafia had drugged him and left him to die in a jungle. With help received in the nick of time, he was saved. Later he rose to the position of the first Indian to be the MD of Pfizer India. Post his retirement from Pfizer, he served as the chairman of the Union Bank of India.

And so, Kewal joined us. While I would prepare all the data for the conversation with the RBI, seeing someone of his stature to lead conversations from our end made a big change in the regulator's comfort level and receptiveness.

Some setbacks notwithstanding, we ended the year on a happy note once again by raising $108 million ($90 million primary + $18 million secondary) in a Series D funding round at a post-money valuation of $900 million—an internal round that saw strong participation by existing investors (sans Sequoia, of course). I deliberately didn't want to hit the unicorn club at this time for a couple of reasons. Firstly, I had the full $75 million from Series C lying untouched and was overcapitalized with $165 million cash in hand. With conversations for a banking licence on, I was certain that with our cash in hand, the RBI would be forced to look at us with more credibility. Secondly, not being in the unicorn club, we could be spared some undue attention from the so-called business journalists whose full-time job now was to ridicule and pull down newly minted unicorns.

While we raised a part of this funding through a primary share sale, the rest was through a secondary share that offered an exit to angel investors as well as ESOP holders. Yes, I gave $18 million cash return by Series D itself to folks who had initially invested $0.3 million. And some of them still continue to hold multimillion-dollar equity stakes in BharatPe, as it has turned out to be the best investment for angel investors in India.

Car Quirk

Speaking of a secondary round, a quirky tale is in order. For those of us who had graduated from IIT Delhi, Deepinder Goyal, the founder of Zomato and a poster boy of the start-up space, was a role model. In fact, in the start-up chronology of things, Deepinder had founded Zomato, from where Albinder had branched off and founded Grofers, and then I had left Grofers to start BharatPe. In terms of start-up lineage, therefore, Deepinder is the grandfather, while I am his grandson. One common passion that runs through Deepinder, Albinder and me is our love for big cars; it's possibly a

Punjabi trait, more so of the Delhi–Chandigarh NH1 belt. When Albinder did a secondary exit, I had seen him and Saurabh Kumar buy Range Rovers. I had also known that Deepinder had bought a new car immediately after every secondary. In fact, when I was at Grofers, Deepinder was selling his BMW Z4, and Albinder had asked me if I wanted to buy it. While I was excited by the proposition, it turned out that Deepinder had traded in his Z4 to buy a brand-new Porsche. I had at that time promised myself that whenever I did a secondary, I would gift myself a car too. True to the promise, just before I got my first $1 million secondary at BharatPe, I bought a second-hand Mercedes-Benz GLS, a seven-seater SUV. I was sold the story that this car, with a Jharkhand number 0005, had earlier been driven by M.S. Dhoni as the brand ambassador of the real estate company that owned it—a story that I never cared to verify.

Having bought this car, a quirk bordering on superstition had settled in my mind that a funding round would only close if I bought a car prior to the round. Inane as this may sound, it is pretty much like how you stand transfixed in an India match, unwilling to change your position that you think made India score in the game. Each of the three cars that I bought during my stint at BharatPe were, therefore, bought before a secondary round closed and before any money actually hit my bank account.

The Maybach, with registration number 0007, came just before Series D, and the Porsche 718 Cayman, with registration number 7180, was bought just before Series E.

All my cars are pre-owned (more value for money) and are funded by my savings on alcohol as a teetotaller. So now you know the recipe to own fancy cars—don't drink or smoke!

11

Martyr to One's Own Cause

'Do you want to bid for a bank?' This question, from Jaspal Bindra, the chairman of the Centrum Group, towards the end of 2020, took me by surprise.

My relationship with Centrum had begun when, having lost the opportunity to handle a large treasury at Grofers, Centrum executives were quick to approach me in the early days of BharatPe. Kotak and Citi, the two banks handling treasury at Grofers, had written me off and were not in touch, theirs being the all-too-common 'kursi ko salaam' attitude. When the Centrum RMs, let's refer to them as Su and Ro, had called on me at BharatPe to handle the initial Rs 1.92 crore that I had raised, I had scoffed and remarked that I was so small that it wouldn't even cover the cab fare that they had incurred in making the visit to my office. Clearly, they had confidence in me, and they were subsequently rewarded with handling our entire treasury, since they were the ones who had been willing to work with me when the business was small. It was along the way of this relationship that I met Jaspal Bindra, their chairman, whose question to me now amounted to fulfilling a commitment that I had made to my investors months earlier.

It turned out that in the wake of the bankruptcy of the corruption-ridden PMC Bank, the RBI had approached the three-decade-old Centrum Group to judge their interest in taking it over. The fraud at PMC Bank had come to light in September 2019, when it was discovered that the bank had allegedly created fictitious accounts to hide bad loans, worth around Rs 7000 crore, to the almost-bankrupt HDIL. The bank had public deposits of more than Rs 10,000 crore, which were at risk, and this was the reason the RBI had put the bank under moratorium. Clearly, the bank was in dire straits and needed a visionary to turn it around.

Jaspal is a celebrated Standard Chartered banker, who acquired a stake in Centrum post his retirement. He, however, knew that no one would bankroll Centrum for the PMC deal and that he would need a partner. I instantly realized that it was a marriage made in heaven. While the RBI would be willing to give the licence to Centrum, I could bring in the money as BharatPe. The fact that we had the experience to convert it into a digital bank made me give my immediate assent to Bindra.

'Play on the front foot,' was my message to him as I agreed to a 50:50 partnership.

In January 2021, we officially put in a bid for PMC. Among the other bidders in the race for the beleaguered bank were two business families from Mumbai and Hyderabad, along with Sanjeev Gupta of the Liberty Group. Besides being the CEO and chairman of an international conglomerate that operated primarily in the steel and mining domain mostly in Africa, Sanjeev Gupta was also expanding the financial service assets in his global business and was the only other contender for the bid. However, Greensill Capital, which was bankrolling the Liberty Group, was declared insolvent in March 2021 in a major scandal, which also led to an investigation involving the prime minister of the United Kingdom. We emerged as the default choice.

While the bidding process was on between January and June 2021, our core business was on an upswing. Not only were we the only fintech doing lending at scale, ours was a de-risked business, as the lending was now being funded not through equity but by other customers' P2P deposits. The bigger story now was that we could become the first fintech that could get a banking licence. By April, I had therefore started preparing for yet another funding round, with this new once-in-a-lifetime opportunity.

While I had planned a fundraising trip to the US for May, India was hit by a deadly COVID wave in March–April 2021. Travelling at this time wasn't the best thing to do, but I knew that this was something that had to be undertaken. Data after the previous COVID wave had shown that UPI adoption had registered a major upswing. It was likely to be no different this time too, and this opportunity had to be seized. Even through the first COVID wave, we had worked without taking a single day off from office. I, in fact, had always been dismissive of COVID. While this had disgruntled some employees, the fact remains that the kind of products we were building wouldn't have been possible had we all not been at work during COVID.

In terms of the team, we now had more people that I could leave the day-to-day working to. In February 2021, I appointed Sumeet Singh, a Shardul Amarchand Mangaldas (SAM) partner, as our general counsel. I had worked with him extensively during the fundraise at Grofers. His first foreign trip was when I took him to Singapore for the Grofers round closure. After I had quit Grofers, Madhuri and I had also driven down to Jaipur for his wedding. Having taken the decision to get a banking licence, I knew that I had to have someone competent in place to handle the legalities. To get him on, however, I not only had to offer him a joining bonus of Rs 80 lakh and CTC of over Rs 1 crore, I also had to offer him ESOPs that would vest in a year. He, in fact, proved to be my hiring mistake Number 3, and the biggest one.

Madhuri, of course, had been handling all administration-related issues, banking operations and vendor payouts that had now increased in scope. She was also handling the treasury through Centrum, besides being in charge of all facilities, building of new offices and more. Post Suhail's joining, I had asked him to allocate budgets to every department. The tracking of these budgets, too, was done by Madhuri. In fact, in a townhall, Suhail had gone on to mention that Madhuri did an extremely critical yet thankless job. Despite her taking on this kind of workload, it was a considered decision that she wasn't appointed a CXO, as both she and I didn't want anyone to ever think that it was because she was the founder's wife that she held the position. We treated the management better than most founders I know. In hindsight, though, it is not something which I would recommend. My experience tells me that you need to keep your management below you fairly and squarely as a founder and that you shouldn't be in a hurry to institutionalize things. In fact, professional competence cannot outweigh loyalty and the ability to take risks.

The one area where I was witnessing some teething issues had to do with Suhail and Jasneet. The two of them were seen hanging out together extensively in the office, along with another colleague, Sahil Chawla from the sales team, who had a nasty reputation for being very political and a gossipmonger. As a CEO designate, Suhail's hanging out with a small coterie of people didn't bode well, as it undermined his position. As for Jasneet, most people, including Bhavik, felt that this association didn't help her in the least to inspire trust among employees. Madhuri, who is generally extremely perceptive about people, also did not have a very good feeling about Jasneet's way of working. I, however, was hoping that as mature professionals, both Suhail and Jasneet would realize this and correct these issues as they settled down in the system. But before leaving for the US trip, I had to ask Sahil to leave, as the situation with the three of them wasn't turning out to be too conducive for the company.

There was yet another strange aspect that Madhuri and I had noted about Suhail. While Suhail would often talk about his wife, Ruchi, no one had ever seen her. He had mentioned that she was his batchmate at IIM Lucknow and worked at the Dalmia Group. However, Ruchi didn't make an appearance at any of our social gatherings or the many dinners that I subsequently hosted for the core team at home. In fact, Madhuri even mentioned to me that it seemed rather odd that there wasn't a single picture of his wife on any of his social media accounts. Since it was clearly his personal area, it wasn't for us to comment, only that it did bring up niggling doubts about his overall character in our minds repeatedly.

Before proceeding to the US, I had clearly laid down the mandate for everybody to work on, in my absence. I had instructed Jasneet to work on building a large tech team, especially since tech hiring was increasingly becoming difficult as start-ups were throwing a lot of money to recruit tech people. I had also instructed Suhail and Bhavik to complete work on two new products, PostPe and 12% Club, which I had envisaged and detailed for them very clearly.

While I was still planning the trip, I got a call from my travel agent, on 28 April, stating that given the worsening COVID situation, the last flight to the US may be in the next few days, and if I needed to go I would have to leave as early as 1 May. I immediately decided to do so. But on 1 May, while Madhuri, the kids and I were at the check-in counter, we heard the announcement that the last flight to the US would be on 4 May.

I had lined up a whole bunch of investor meetings, beginning 8 May, in the US, having kept the intervening days for a self-quarantine. For this reason, we didn't go directly to my sister-in-law's house but opted to stay in an Airbnb for the first few days.

Importantly, I wanted to make sure that we got vaccinated the next day after landing in the US.

Tiger, Tiger Burning Bright

Prior to my visit, I had already sent my pitch deck out to all investors, especially since our bank bid looked more promising. One of the investors that I was very keen to bring on our cap table was Tiger Global. I had interacted with the Tiger Global team closely when I was at Grofers. While the general perception in the Indian market about them was that they went by their own whims and fancies—'*jispar Scott ka dil aa jata hai uspar paise laga dete hain ek phone call par* (if Scott has his heart on you as a founder, Tiger comes in quickly and big)'—however, I knew that they were the right partners for our business. I had met Scott Shleifer, partner at Tiger Global, earlier, while he was visiting Delhi in 2019. He had just flown in from Beijing when I met him, as late as 10 p.m. at the Oberoi, Delhi, where he was staying. Totally jetlagged, he was literally swaying while I explained our business model to him for over an hour. While he heard me out, given that he was so jetlagged, I wasn't sure how much of it he had absorbed.

At that time Tiger had already invested in OkCredit, a digital ledger and bookkeeping app. I recall explaining to Scott that OkCredit and Khata Book may have become popular as bookkeeping apps, but lending couldn't be done on the back of unverified bookkeeping. I even opened the Khata Book app and demonstrated to him that there was an entry that showed thousands of crores owed to me by an entry named Mukesh Ambani. That clearly didn't mean that money could be lent to me on the premise that Mukesh Ambani owed me the crores that were showing in my Khata Book. If anything, it only showed that the app was such a novice that it had not even put limiters on the zeros one could put. While in the US economy an 'I owe you' may be enough, in India, I explained, enforcing receivables under legal contracts is a long process at courts. Moneylending in India, therefore, was feasible only when you were in the cashflow of the person you were lending to. In fact, if bookkeeping could justify lending, VCs/PE should be putting money into Tally (owned by the Ambanis, incidentally), which carries the entire country's ledgers. I couldn't, however, fathom how much of my argument Scott was buying.

I had another meeting with Scott in November 2019, when I was visiting New York. This time, we were meeting in his gorgeous office, located in the heart of Manhattan, overlooking Central Park. We were joined by one of his colleagues, Alex Cook. Having put the money in OkCredit and already being a legacy investor in PhonePe, because of residual stake in Flipkart, Cook was dismissive of our business. Once Scott entered the room, however, the entire vibe changed. To my surprise, for a full fifteen minutes, he explained to Cook how he had met me in New Delhi earlier that year and even went on to describe verbatim the nuances of our business as I had explained to him in our last meeting, one where he was visibly jetlagged. While Cook didn't seem very convinced, Scott even invited his public-side fintech analyst, who had evaluated the model of Square Inc. in the US, a company that put POS machines at shops and was getting into the small-business-lending space. While our deal didn't go through, my respect for Scott grew manifold during that meeting.

This time, though, I was scheduled to meet Alex and Scott on a Zoom call. While Alex turned up for the meeting in the morning, Scott didn't. I was disappointed to say the least and saw it as a sign of their lack of interest. Adding just a small glimmer of hope, the meeting was rescheduled for the same afternoon. Logging on to that Zoom meeting, I nearly felt that I had entered the portals of heaven. There was Scott, sitting in pristine white clothes, with his shiny pate and everything around him extremely bright. While I would have had an opportunity to just about say hi, he undertook a monologue on how I was building a great business and that they were convinced that what BharatPe was doing PhonePe wouldn't be able to achieve. Interestingly, Scott used the F-word twenty-eight times in that conversation. At the end of that call, Scott indicated that he wanted to put in $100 million in our business and was willing to offer a valuation of $3 billion. All this while, Alex Cook's expression conveyed that Scott was overselling. On noticing his expression, Scott went on to say that he would, of course, be much happier if I were to price the round closer to $2.5 billion.

It was clearly a big win, one that was achieved through a lot of hard work. Even when Tiger Global wasn't on my cap table, I used to diligently send them our monthly updates, for them to witness our growth story at first hand. They weren't just any other investor, rather one that enabled founders to fly. What had also struck me about Tiger was their diligence. While at Grofers, I had seen them doing a lot of on-ground work, such as analysing our app store reviews, reviewing our NPS score, talking to customers on the ground and more, some of the work which, as founders, even we may not have done.

With Tiger's commitment, the rest of the investor meetings were a cakewalk. With a lead investor of the scale of Tiger Global, all I had to do was to tell the others that Tiger was leading the round with $100 million. In San Francisco for three weeks, I made it a point to meet nearly ten investors a week while also visiting New York to meet some investors there as well.

The incredible part of this fundraise was that whereas I wanted to raise $250 million, I had signed offers for $625 million, including internal investors vying for more than their pro rata share. This fundraise also had Sequoia participating once again through their growth fund, having sat out on the Series C and D rounds. It was inconceivable that I was having to say no to marquee investors willing to put in $255 million while raising a total round of $370 million–$350 million through primary infusion and $20 million through secondary buyout.

ICC, Bush's Son-in-Law, Quiche and a Lot More

As early as December 2020, I had made the decision for BharatPe to become a sponsor of the ICC World Cup. As opposed to the Indian Premier League (IPL), this property was far more economical and uncluttered, and I wanted to use it to build the brand. I used to have a lot of media sales guys visiting me in order to sell the IPL property. However, I found the space extremely cluttered. The number of logos on the team jerseys alone was mind-boggling. I remember making an offer to have the BharatPe logo along with our QR code on the player's bum, the only space the IPL franchises hadn't already sold. While the ad sales guy thought that I wasn't being serious, I was only half-joking. Had they allowed it, they would have had us on board.

In December 2020, however, I cracked a deal with the International Cricket Council (ICC). While they had two kinds of sponsorships on offer—global (higher) and official (lower)—BharatPe, or one of our group brands interchangeably, offered to be the global sponsors for the first and third years (which would have covered both T20 and ODI World Cups originally scheduled for India), and the official sponsor for the second year (T20 World Cup in Australia) at $27 million. Their first event was the ICC World Test Championship, and I decided to go and watch the five-day India–New Zealand match at Southampton on my way back from the US.

I was invited by a good friend, Bhavin Turakhia, a serial entrepreneur who, along with his brother, ranks among the richest people in India, to stay at his house in central London. With the UK having strict quarantine rules at that time, I thought it would be far more convenient to stay with him, as opposed to staying in a COVID hotel; and so I took him up on his kind offer. The UK had a rule at the time, whereby you had to quarantine for ten days, test yourself on the second as well as the eighth day from landing and report your test results. You could also do an additional test on Day 5 to come out of quarantine earlier. I found this test illogical—if on the second day I am negative, then, clearly, I haven't brought COVID with me, and there should ideally be no further quarantine. With governments, though, logic does not work, and I think the UK government wanted to deter tourists or perhaps make some money to cover the National Health Service (NHS) costs.

Bhavin's house is a luxurious four-storey townhouse right behind Oxford Street, and we were given a whole floor. A day after landing, while we were supposed to self-quarantine, the kids were quite restless and wanted to step out. On our landing, we already had test kits for the second-day test delivered to us. I happened to click pictures of these test kits and proceeded to take the kids out to Hyde Park. While we were in the park, I received a call from the NHS, wanting to confirm that we were quarantining. Hearing the kids screaming in the park in the background, the lady asked me to read out the bar codes of the test kits that we would have received, to make sure that we were indeed homebound. Thankfully, I could pass that test because of the pictures on my phone, but that was enough of a scare for us to rush back to Bhavin's house.

The next day, Bhavin's brother, Divyank, was scheduled to also fly into London. The butler informed us that the police officials had visited the house even before Divyank had reached from the airport to inquire if he was quarantining, a fact that had us surprised. The next morning, we happened to meet Divyank and his girlfriend briefly. A day later we were joined by another gentleman in the house. When we met him, he was enjoying a well-laid-out breakfast in the central courtyard. I quickly introduced myself as Bhavin's friend and, by way of conversation, asked him what he did, to which he replied that he made animated films for Netflix. This piqued my son's curiosity, who went on to ask if he made cartoons, but on being told that his content was for adults, he quickly lost interest. Madhuri, however, noticed that from us, being the original guests in the place, the butler's attention was now totally focused on this gentleman. That attention showed in the spinach quiche and the exotic fruits that this gentleman was having and that our friendly butler did not offer to us that morning. Not happy with this arrangement, Madhuri, in jest, went and sat on the empty seat between me and the gentleman, and tore a piece of the quiche and helped herself to it. The gentleman nearly apologized for not offering it to us himself.

It was only on the last day, when we were to leave and I went to thank Divyank for his hospitality, that he asked me if I had had the chance to spend time with his friend. On my stating that I had only briefly met him, he told me that the gentleman's name was Craig Coyne, and that he was married to Barbara Bush, a name that didn't ring a bell with me; however, I did fathom that he was someone fairly important. By this time, Madhuri and the kids were already in the car, as we were shifting to Madhuri's friend's place for the next few days. As soon as I reached the car I joked to Madhuri, '*Tune zaroor kuch panga kiya hai* (What have you done now?),' and asked her to quickly google Craig Coyne, the gentleman whose quiche she had unceremoniously eaten. Sure enough, it turned out that the gentleman in question was former US President George Bush's son-in-law. That explained the butler's comment about the police coming in the day they had landed—in all probability, it was the Secret Service checking in on his arrival.

Having arrived at Madhuri's friend's place and scheduled to watch the match, I received a call as early as 7 a.m. that was game-changing. 'We have won the PMC bid,' said Jaspal Bindra, to my jubilation. Officially, we were the only fintech in the country now with a banking licence. While New Zealand beat India to make history in the match, the loss didn't seem that crushing any more. I had made history already!

Back Home

Back at work, I was in for some not-so-pleasant developments. Turns out that while I was heavy-lifting in the US and raising money on the promise of new products, no work had happened in the interim on PostPe as well as 12% Club. 'I need to speak to you but not in the office,' Bhavik answered when I asked him about what was transpiring. His explanation, when he met me at my home, was, '*Tech team udd gayi hai.*' A large part of the tech team had resigned. The tech team, which had sixty-odd people when I left, was now apparently down to forty. Bhavik went on to add that hiring wasn't his ballgame.

When I asked what Jasneet was doing, his reply shocked me. 'Jasneet and Suhail are seeing each other. In fact, Suhail has moved in with her. The atmosphere at work is quite unhealthy,' he said. I was absolutely certain that Jasneet needed to go. Dhruv, our COO, informed me that if I asked Jasneet to go at this time, I could save ESOPs worth Rs 1 crore that would soon be vested. I, however, didn't want any drama at a time when the company was on the brink of operationalizing a bank takeover and closure of Series E. It's another matter that as soon as her ESOPs vested and encashed in the secondary, she put in her resignation the very next week. Madhuri's early reading of Jasneet had come true. 'Did you know that Jasneet had resigned? I didn't know,' Suhail had the temerity to say to me after her resignation. I was quite taken aback that while the entire organization knew of their affair, I was to believe that Suhail didn't know of her resignation. While I let that pass, I was now certain that I was dealing with someone who couldn't be relied upon.

The bigger issue for me at the time was getting the tech team in place. I spent the next three months running around building the tech team. I first ensured that mid-year appraisals were done on priority and additional ESOPs offered to retain the remaining tech team. That done, I had to do something quite drastic to get new members on board. Apparently, the conversion rates on our tech interviews were very poor. I was told that Cred had a good conversion rate. On probing further, I found that when Cred gave out an offer letter, it also gave the prospective employee a laptop. I knew we had to better the offer. Our hiring commercials worked as follows: the average engineer salary was Rs 20 lakh per annum; we were also paying nearly Rs 3 lakh to headhunters as commission over and above this. I knew instantly that we had to make these Rs 3 lakh count.

One of our sales guys, Karan, was a passionate biker. My next pit stop was to him to ask him which fancy bike could Rs 3 lakh fetch. On his revert, that Rs 3 lakh could get us a BMW bike in addition to the usual KTM or Royal Enfield, I knew I had a winning formula. With most young techies secretly lusting for superbikes, this was bound to work. All we needed to do was to put a small creative up on LinkedIn for it to become viral. The entire industry was buzzing with the news that BharatPe was giving away superbikes to their tech joinees. While several founders personally cursed me for spoiling the recruitment market, I strongly believe that I had anticipated what could otherwise have become a big issue and had nipped it in the bud. I was already hearing from my counterparts in the US that finding engineers was becoming extremely tough. In fact, fintech founders there were struggling as engineers from companies like Google and Facebook were looking at $1 million salaries. This clearly was one way to buck the tide without any commercial hit. The fact that we had a one-year lock-in period for anyone who joined and availed the bike was an added advantage.

Besides, I also promised that the entire tech team could work out of Dubai (where the T20 World Cup was moved from India—thanks to the COVID scare) up until the World Cup, which we were sponsoring and which I had passes for. There clearly was no reason for engineers not to join BharatPe. While the competition blew all this out of proportion and termed it as 'blowing investors' money', it was anything but that. Not only were we killing it in terms of recruitment, the move had also gone a long way in building BharatPe's brand as an employer.

On the product side, I next launched PostPe, a buy-now-pay-later service, with the ICC T20 World Cup in Dubai. I had taken ownership of it from Suhail as I had not seen anything move in the two months that I'd been away. The app allows consumers to avail credit of up to Rs 10 lakh. With PostPe, one can pay anywhere using QR or card, or by directly taking money into their bank account. PostPe ensures that consumers can make not just big-ticket purchases but also micro-purchases on EMI, making it a first-of-its-kind product. '*Mujhe gol gappe EMI pe bechne hai* (I want everyday purchases, such as street food, to be sold on monthly instalments), without the need for a card machine.' This was my drive behind launching PostPe.

The foray into the consumer space continued with 12% Club, which enables people to either lend or borrow at a flat 12 per cent annualized interest, making it the only zero-spread product in the world. Through this app, we raised a lot of money that got deployed towards merchant loans. While the cost of capital here was 12 per cent, the IRR from the merchant lending piece was as high as 48 per cent. We were clearly earning 6–7x of what the best of NBFCs earned as spread. Both the products were instant hits and shook the fintech market.

Dubai Sojourn

By the beginning of the ICC World Cup, almost the entire tech team had been stationed in Dubai. The idea also was to hold them there until Diwali to prevent poaching, quite like hoarding Indian legislators in resorts to prevent them from defecting to the other side. I had entrusted Madhuri with all the arrangements for everyone's travel and stay. Additionally, we offered each member of the team 3750 dirhams (roughly Rs 80,000), so that they didn't feel that while their earnings were in Indian currency, they were spending in dirhams. Post finishing their work in the day, they could all go out to see the match in the evening. In fact, for the much-anticipated India–Pakistan match, I also flew down the rest of the core team to Dubai. Madhuri negotiated a good package with the Taj hotels. We even booked a presidential suite, where everyone could lounge after the matches.

By this time, though, we hadn't paid ICC any money. This is because, for an overseas sporting event, an approval needs to be sought from the Ministry of Youth Affairs and Sports. This approval, for some reason, was delayed, for us as well as for Byju's. While Suhail and Sumeet were explaining the technicality to the organizers, ICC wanted my personal word that the money would be remitted. We had committed a sum of nearly Rs 200 crore for three years, but we would have had to pay an additional Rs 36 crore as GST on remittance from India. It was at this time that Madhuri suggested that, given the fact that Madhuri and I had been offered a Golden Visa by the Dubai government, we set up a subsidiary of BharatPe in Dubai. If the amount from BharatPe could be transferred to this subsidiary company, which in turn could pay ICC, there was no approval required on remittance and no GST incidence. ICC was happy with this arrangement. In fact, ICC agreed to net off the 5 per cent VAT if we paid through the Dubai subsidiary. By creating this structure, Madhuri ended up saving US$5 million for the business.

That sorted, the grand finale of the Dubai trip came by way of a boat ride that I had organized for some core members of the team. The boat belonged to Bhavin Turakhia, who had very graciously offered it to me for use while I was in Dubai. We were in for a surprise here too. For Suhail came accompanied by Tarana Lalwani of InnoVen Capital, a company through which we had done wholesale borrowings. While there had been some gossip about people having spotted them together on earlier occasions and about their making frequent trips with each other, for them to make an appearance at an official do was a bit of a surprise for everyone. This especially when Suhail had mentioned that his supposed wife would also be joining us on the Dubai trip, which of course didn't happen. On my subsequent Dubai trip, too, I happened to chance upon Suhail, unaware of the reason he was in Dubai.

A Fatal Mistake

In hindsight, this was the time I made an error in judgement, one that I had to pay for dearly. Bhavik and I were in Mumbai along with Suhail and Sumeet, for a meeting with Jaspal Bindra, post winning the bank licence. At night, while I crashed in my room, the rest of them continued to drink in Bhavik's room. The next morning, Bhavik wanted to share something with me. 'People have a lot of angst against Madhuri,' he said, to my surprise. On my probing him, he said that they do not want to be accountable to her on the budgets as she isn't a CXO. "If Madhuri is given a board seat, I will quit by March," Suhail said to us last night,' Bhavik reported to me.

Between Shashvat and me as founders, we had four board seats. I had thought that we would give one board seat to Suhail and the other to Madhuri. While I was shocked to hear Suhail's statement, as I was going out of my way to promote him, I decided against ruffling many feathers at the growth stage of the business. On the basis of this feedback, therefore, I decided to keep the fourth board seat open. In fact, after the fundraise closed, I went on to appoint Suhail as the CEO along with appointing him to the board.

'Hope you have thought this decision through,' Micky Malka said to me on a phone call. Micky went on to call for a board meeting to get me to reiterate to the board that my elevating Suhail as the CEO and putting him on the board would not dilute my responsibility to BharatPe, and that I would be the *karta-dharta*. According to him, their money was riding on me, and they did not care about Suhail. In hindsight, this was the time I should have appointed Madhuri to the board. It was my board seat, not of the management or investors, and I had the sole right to decide on it. Clearly, Suhail had no business to tell me whom he would share the board seat with. At my end, I was blinded by the company's growth and deliveries as opposed to protecting my own interests. As a friend rightly put it once the entire saga had unfolded, 'You were doing what was right for the business, but *tune apni bali chadha di* (you became a martyr to your own cause).'

12

Shark Tank

My private Instagram account, without the coveted blue tick, had all of 285 followers when we wrapped up the *Shark Tank India* shoot in Film City. I was, in turn, following 315 people. When I agreed to be on the first season of the show, to even think that this would be an iconic television show that would propel a rather shy individual into becoming a national youth icon, and that I would have my 'following' jump through the roof on social media, seemed farfetched. Yet this was exactly what *Shark Tank* did for me. Or what I did for *Shark Tank*!

One of my initial angel investors was Venture Catalysts. They were assisting the team at *Shark Tank India* to identify a panel of 'Sharks', and it was they who recommended my name. To be aired on Sony Television, *Shark Tank* was a popular, international-format show on which investors or 'Sharks' are pitched to, by business owners who are looking for funding. Interestingly enough, I had never really seen a full episode of *Shark Tank US*, even though I was aware of its format.

As early as July 2021, I was on a Zoom call with a gentleman called Bimal Unnikrishnan, the showrunner for *Shark Tank*. The call was followed up with a recording session set up at my home, which involved some mock pitches made by the Sony team, to which I had to respond impromptu.

As I saw Sony's interest growing, I realized that if the association went through, it would turn me into a public figure of sorts. I was a bit apprehensive, as in the middle of hectic business deliverables, I didn't want my investors to think *'Ashneer distract ya vela ho gaya hai'*, that Ashneer has time for things outside business. I remember writing to Micky Malka, seeking his view. His response was matter-of-fact: in short, he said that while he personally wouldn't want people to recognize him as he walked down a street, that was just the way he was. Post Micky's 'you do you' message, I reached out to Harshjit at Sequoia, who also didn't have any strong views against it. I was good to go.

Yet another mock session with Sony followed. This session had two likely but yet unconfirmed Sharks: Aman Gupta, the co-founder of BoAt and myself. While the Sony team wanted to keep the session in a hotel, I told them there was no need to waste money and that I was happy to offer my home for it. This was the first time I was meeting Aman. I remember thinking that he was filled with a kind of nervous energy. *Usko* Shark Tank *chahiye tha*, he really wanted to be on the *Shark Tank* panel. In fact, it meant far more to him than it did to me at that time.

They screened with the two of us together. Post the screening, while we were having rajma chawal for lunch, I was asked by Aman, *'Ashneer Bhai, kya lagta hai, lenge ya nahi* (Do you think they will select us)?' To my nonchalant *'Kya farak padta hai* (How does it matter)?' came his impassioned, *'Maine* Shark Tank *dekh kar dhandha banaya hai* (I have grown up watching *Shark Tank* and was inspired by it to build my own business).' This was the first time I realized that being on the show could indeed mean something big.

The one thing that was extremely important to me was finding out who the other co-panellists would be, should I be on the show. I let Madhuri lead the conversations with the Sony team. She, of course, quickly realized that the show could have a big value beyond our immediate start-up circles and was convinced that I should be on it. On speaking to Bimal, she was informed about the other likely co-panellists. Of these, Anupam Mittal, of Shaadi.com, was someone I had myself pitched earlier to during our seed round. While he was keen to invest, by then Sequoia had agreed to put in money, so I hadn't pursued his investment any further. The dosa seller in his office canteen had the BharatPe QR, and he would often call me directly for any service he needed. As for the others, while I hadn't met Peyush Bansal of Lenskart, I had high regard for the business he had built. The fact that he had also raised money from SoftBank made me happy to share the stage with a SoftBank investee–founder. I had already met Aman and knew of his success in building a D2C brand. As we went along, I got to know that Vineeta Singh, of Sugar Cosmetics, would be on the show. She was one year junior to me at IIM, and while we had never really spoken on campus, we knew of each other and had mutual respect for the businesses we had built. The one person I didn't know was Namita Thapar of Emcure Pharmaceuticals, and I'd had no common episodes with Ghazal Alagh, co-founder of Mama Earth—but their credentials were equally impressive. Overall, I was happy that I was sharing the stage with some great operating founders and not some 'gyaan pelne vale' investors or angels.

That didn't, however, take away my apprehension at being on television. It was not natural for me. I had never been a public speaker. I remember how my legs would shake when I had to read the morning news in the school assembly in front of hundreds of students. I was in two minds even on the weekend that I had to travel for the first shoot. Once I was on the set, however, I experienced extremely positive vibes. In true celebrity style, we had our own vanity vans and full entourage—make-up people, costume designers, bouncers, even someone who would hold an umbrella for you while you walked towards the set. To say that we felt extremely important would be an understatement; we felt truly pampered.

Of course, so much importance comes at a price, and I had to pay it with the wrath of my wife, Madhuri, who accompanied me for all the shoots without fail. In a rather funny episode on the very first day of our shoot, while I was still in my vanity van, a young girl, the costume designer's assistant, walked up to me to innocuously ask me, *'Ashneer Sir, kapde aa gaye hain. Pehna doon* (Your clothes are here. Should I help you wear them)?' She hadn't anticipated that the vanity van had yet another occupant, my rather possessive wife. Not only did Madhuri ask the girl to wait outside while I got dressed, she even went up to Bimal to tell him that he shouldn't be giving us so much importance. *'Chane ke jhaad par mat chadhao inhe'* were her exact words. She explained that we were not big industrialists, just normal middle-class boys and that we should be kept grounded. She even went on to tell him that our staff should be reduced and that for male Sharks, they should stick to male costume dadas.

Lo and behold, the very next day our staff was reduced to half, to the shock of all the Sharks. Aman was quite upset and even asked Madhuri, *'Aap sab shoots par aaoge kya* (Will you come for all the shoots)?' When Madhuri replied in the affirmative, he walked me to the side with a plea to do something about it. *'Ashneer Bhai, kuch karo, sara glamour hi khatam ho gaya hai* (Ashneer, do something, the whole charm of shooting is gone),' he said in his characteristic style.

Speaking of clothes, this was actually one of the causes of our angst at *Shark Tank*. Our clothes were repeated so much that one feedback from the audience was, *'Ameer ho, kapde toh badal lo* (You are rich enough to be able to afford more clothes).' But the team was unsure which episodes would finally be aired, and about the editing around it and the continuity of the episodes, and hence people saw us week after week sporting the same set of clothes.

Shark Tank had a huge set, which had reportedly cost them Rs 4.5 crore to build. It was built by the same set designer who had built the set for the much-talked-about *Koffee with Karan*. The set was so huge that we didn't know what the other Sharks or contestants were saying except through our earpieces. As opposed to the popular belief that everything on reality shows is scripted, there was nothing scripted at *Shark Tank*. We didn't even know how many pitches were being made on a particular day or which companies were pitching. Every week, we would be shooting for three days, including the weekend.

I had, at the very beginning, committed to all dates except for one week when I needed to be in Dubai for the ICC T20 World Cup final. Week after week, we would travel to Mumbai, either on Thursday night to be back on Sunday, or travel on Friday to return on Monday. With Peyush, Aman, Madhuri and me taking the flight from Delhi every week, we had become good friends and would often be seen pulling each other's leg. At the airport, Aman would often take off his mask and walk around to see if anyone recognized him, while we made sure to rub it in by saying, '*Tereko koi nahi jaanta* (Nobody recognizes you).' While we spent long, hectic hours on the set, often from as early as 8 a.m. to 10 p.m., we had all developed a great camaraderie with each other as co-judges. The bonding was especially forged over some delicacies that Namita would bring from her company guesthouse for us to gorge on.

Amid this camaraderie, there was only one run-in with a fellow Shark. My style on *Shark Tank*, as also in life, was to be absolutely honest (read: blunt) in making my views known. Some people even went on to point out the similarities between my stance and that of a Shark on the American show. But the fact is that I hadn't clicked on any of the links that Bimal and his team had sent to me as references from the American show. *Main apni tarah kar raha tha*, I was simply being myself. I recall Bimal coming up to me after the first few episodes' shoots to warn me, '*Pehle teri pitai hogi but baad mein people will love you* (You will be hated first, and then you will be loved).' In those early days of the shoot, Bimal even asked me if I wanted any portions edited. I was clear that I had said what I had because I believed in it. I therefore gave him full freedom to carry whatever he wanted.

Things panned out exactly as Bimal had predicted. The first week of the show being aired was especially tough for me—I was getting up even in the middle of the night to read the negative comments on my now freshly blue-ticked official Instagram handle. It is another matter that the hatred accrued as much from my no-holds-barred feedback to pitchers on *Shark Tank* as from the BharatPe drama that had begun to unfold by then. People had no idea about the way the boardroom politics was panning out, but that didn't stop fake accounts with zero posts and followers proclaiming '*Tu chor hai saale, Kotak vale ko gaali kyun di* (Why did you abuse the Kotak guy on the call)?' on my social media handles.

The next week onwards, however, there was a polarization, with a lot of people feeling that I was being true to the task at hand, as there was no point praising a contestant's business model while denying him funding. People also seemed to warm up to my Hindi-speaking persona that was closely rooted in ground realities. In fact, I soon realized that a lot of my following came from businesspeople, while I wasn't the working-class, English-speaking guy's favourite. To put it succinctly, *main measured ya politically correct bande ka banda hi nahi hoon*, I am not one who puts a premium on being measured over being honest.

My run-in with a co-Shark was also on this count. Turns out that on one occasion, Namita thought that I was way too blunt to a contestant. Her views were welcome, of course, except instead of airing them to me, she chose to share them with the other Sharks. The only reason I could hear them was because I was still wearing my earpiece. Not one to mince words, I confronted her and told her that it would work well if she spoke to me directly. Of course, we made up the very next day as I went and hugged her, telling her that I wasn't offended by what she had said, only by the fact that she hadn't chosen to speak directly to me. That cleared the air between us.

The first week was also rough on another count. The contestants knew Aman and Vineeta on account of the consumer-facing D2C brands that they had built, and this meant many of them were naturally inclined towards them. That meant that even if the other Sharks were offering attractive deals, the pitchers placed a premium on these Sharks as investors, hoping they would get operational help in building their businesses. One of the episodes that became quite famous was the one where I expressed my displeasure to the founder of Bummer, a comfort wear brand. That was the culmination of a lot of pitches that I had sat through, where the contestants seemed enamoured of the D2C Sharks as opposed to evaluating the deal on its own merit. After that episode, I was told that word had spread among contestants that '*Ashneer se bach kar rehna* (beware of Ashneer)'.

When Kiara Advani Almost Got Me Divorced

While the Bollywood actress Kiara Advani had nothing to do with *Shark Tank*, she was the one-point agenda in one of my shoot travels. Turns out that since I was shooting weekend after weekend and spending the rest of the week at work, my mom hadn't had a chance to talk to me for a long time. I was scheduled to travel again that evening when she remarked to me in jest, '*Bahot bada aadmi ho gaya hai, nazar hi nahi aata* (You have become too big, I don't get to see you now).' Just that morning, a friend, who is also a start-up founder, had dropped by at our office. In a casual conversation, Madhuri and I had asked him if marriage was on the cards for him, and he had nonchalantly mentioned, '*Kisi movie star se baat chal rahi hai* (Talks are on with a movie star).' We were very intrigued by this Bollywood angle. On probing further, he said that there was a Seema Aunty kind of matchmaker, who specialized in Bollywood alliances. When I asked him who his options were, he mentioned Kiara Advani as an eligible match. To my mother's jibe on my having become very big, I laughed and said, '*Aap ko pata nahi hai market mein aaj kal kya chal raha hai. Aaj ke din shaadi ho rahi hoti na toh Kiara Advani ka rishta aata aapke bete ke liye* (You don't know what is happening in the market these days. If I was to get married now, I could be marrying Kiara Advani).'

Madhuri's face fell on hearing this—she did not find the conversation funny at all. I could see an instant change in her body language. We were to travel to Mumbai for the shoot that night. On the aircraft, Madhuri sat tight-lipped and wouldn't speak to me, until they served food and I nagged her to eat it. It was as if a sudden dam had burst. '*Tumhe Kiara Advani se shaadi karni hai* (You want to marry Kiara Advani)?' she raged, beginning to take off her jewellery. Here I was, caught totally off guard. For the next half an hour, I was blasted by her about how I was a nobody when she married me and that I was also on *Shark Tank* on her prodding. Through this tirade I sat with my hands held out, holding her jewellery, which she had unceremoniously dumped on me. From the corner of my eye, I could see an old gentleman who had his headphones on to watch a Netflix movie take them off to listen in on the live movie playing out on the aircraft. This was probably the best flight for the business class co-passengers, with live entertainment.

On landing, when I told this story to my fellow Sharks, I had unwittingly given them a lot of fodder for leg-pulling.

* * *

After all the fun of shooting the episodes, the airing of *Shark Tank India* was a mixed bag for me. Of course, there was huge public recognition; my social media accounts swelled over, with more than 7,00,000 organic followers, not to mention the fact that I had become one of the most meme-worthy individuals. Everywhere I stepped out, there were demands for pictures. Gone was the person who would be extremely conscious around strangers or of being in front of a camera. What I particularly liked was when people walked up to me to say that, inspired by me on *Shark Tank*, they had gone on to either set up a successful business or grow their existing business. That the reason for my being known among people was entrepreneurship, my first love, made it extremely special. The other thing I had managed to achieve was to take the sheen off English as a language for large, organized businesses. In fact, I feel that it is often used as a veil to hide behind, when it comes to non-delivery. What I had done instead was to normalize the use of Hindi in transacting business.

All this, however, coincided with the high drama that was unfolding at BharatPe, and a bloodbath was playing out in full public view. It was an extremely tough time for me. While I felt guilty about hijacking attention from my fellow Sharks and even from the show, because of the controversy that was brewing, personally, this was one of the most challenging periods of my life. It was ironic that the organization that I had built brick by brick was being wrested out of my own hands by the very people I had trusted, at a time when the public at large was lauding me for my entrepreneurial skills.

When the entire episode played out, some people even asked me if my appearance in *Shark Tank* had led to the huge drama and my downfall. Well, whether or not that was the case, I have no regrets about having been a part of *Shark Tank*. There is no denying that the show gave me a public identity. Mixed with other aspects it became a deadly concoction, but that is quite another story.

If there was one thing that I was sure of even in the midst of the bloodbath, it was that try as they might, it would be impossible for them to make the spirits of this Shark sink!

13

The Nykaa IPO and Kotak Saga

23 July 2021

'*Sir, 116 par khula hai share* (The share has listed at 116).'

'Sell.'

'*Mujhe aapko recorded line par lena hoga* (I will have to take you on a recorded line).'

The share price was rising in the interim.

'Order executed at Rs 136 per share.'

Within eight minutes of the Zomato IPO opening, I had made over Rs 2.25 crore.

* * *

I had invested most of the secondary sale considerations that I got in the Series C, D and E rounds back in other start-ups. No surprise there because, for an early-to-bed teetotaller, I really had no other major expenses. One thing was clear: creating a stock market public equity portfolio was not for me. I have been certain that if you hedge your bets, you get mediocre returns. What excites me is putting money behind high-risk early-stage founders. In fact, I had begun this journey early, investing in promising companies like Bira (yeah, despite being a teetotaller) even while I was with Grofers. At BharatPe, my risk appetite increased, and I not only invested in individual companies but also in two US-based tech funds: Ribbit, my investor at BharatPe, and a new fund called Left Lane Capital, started by Vinny Pujji when he was all of twenty-eight years old. Pujji had, of course, reposed his early trust in BharatPe while at Insight Partners.

The year 2021 was also a time when a lot of private tech companies were getting listed through IPOs. By this time, Ro and Su, my wealth management RMs at Centrum, had moved to Kotak. While I now had an ongoing relationship with Centrum, since they wanted to cover me at Kotak, I did my IPO investments through them. I told them that I would invest in only four IPOs which had very strong fundamentals: Zomato, Delhivery, Nykaa and PolicyBazaar.

I was bullish on the Zomato IPO on several counts. Of course, I knew of Deepinder, and I am a big believer in his ability to persevere and keep building big. Fundamentally, with the pandemic the ticket size of their orders had grown, as people were ordering food from home for 3–4 members in the family, as against single rolls in office, thereby increasing Zomato's absolute margins. Moreover, with restaurants completely dependent during lockdowns on app orders, there was no risk of the take-rate coming down. On the other hand, job insecurity among delivery boys kept delivery costs in check. In fact, COVID magically solved the food delivery economics in the country overnight, just like it skyrocketed UPI penetration.

When I put in an application worth Rs 100 crore for the Zomato IPO, everyone was blown away by how I had found that kind of money. It was, however, a case of simple leverage—IPO financing. While I invested Rs 5 crore from my pocket, Kotak

Wealth got me a financing for Rs 95 crore at an interest rate of 10 per cent annualized for a week (the period for which IPO funds get blocked). This cost of Rs 20 lakh as interest was an additional cost for acquiring the shares.

With the IPO being oversubscribed more than thirty times, I got an allotment of shares worth over Rs 3 crore. My RMs, based on grey-market premiums, were expecting the Zomato share to list between Rs 85–90, as against an issue price of Rs 76. I, however, was certain that it would do far better. When the share opened on the listing day at Rs 116 per share, I mandated them to sell all my shares. By the time the trade got executed, I got a selling price of Rs 136 per share. With my landing cost after interest being between Rs 82–85, I ended up making over Rs 2.25 crore. A little greedy post the Zomato IPO, I went in for the Car Trade IPO but ended up losing Rs 25 lakh there.

By October 2021 it was time for the big-ticket Nykaa IPO. I knew at the outset that it would be a super-duper hit. Not only had I worked under Falguni Nayyar at Kotak and knew of her capabilities, but I also had common investors with Nykaa in Steadview, who spoke very highly of her business.

Just before I was scheduled to travel for the *Shark Tank* shoot to Mumbai on 27 October, the guys at Kotak sent me the loan documents for IPO financing. A total of some 200 pages. I remember signing them laboriously in my Malviya Nagar office and even telling the guys at Kotak that there surely should be an easier, digital way of doing these signatures: '*Ye papers waise bhi chhuhe khayenge* (In any case, these papers would be a feast for some rodents at some point).' There were some pages that you even had to sign multiple times. I could never understand the point of multiple signatures—other than to remind you that taking a loan shouldn't be easy.

After landing in Mumbai, I headed straight for a meeting with General Atlantic, where I received a call from Madhuri.

'There are some additional documents that the Kotak guys
are sending through their rider, that they want you to sign,'
she said. Before entering my meeting at a restaurant in BKC,
I remember sitting under the guard's umbrella outside and
signing the additional set of papers. The IPO was supposed
to open the next day, i.e. 28 October. It was while I was in
the vanity van, getting ready for the *Shark Tank* shoot later in
the day, that Madhuri came up to me to tell me that she had
just been informed by our RMs that Kotak was not financing
the Nykaa IPO. I found it extremely surprising. Not only was
Falguni ex-Kotak, but the IPO was expected to do extremely
well. Why on earth would Kotak not finance it? I immediately
called up my RM Ro to ask what the issue was. 'The market
isn't doing that well. Even if we get some money, it may be all
of Rs 20 crore. It's not worth it,' was his nonchalant reply. 'Why
did you get 500 pages signed by me if you all weren't financing
this IPO?' I asked, but my query was met with no conclusive
answer, except they informed me that no Kotak customer had
received this financing.

Not convinced, I asked Madhuri to check with Suhail, since
I knew for a fact that he had also applied for leverage. 'I have
got Rs 20 crore of financing,' was Suhail's reply to Madhuri.
That had me worked up—the Kotak executive was spinning a
different story. My calls to the RMs this time were to ask them
some very pointed questions as to why they were lying when
financing was indeed being offered to others. Their reply this
time was also as unconvincing as the first time, as they now
tried to tell me that there might be some other group within
the wealth management team at Kotak that had been able to
get some funding. Quite surprised by their casual attitude and
blatant lies, I reminded them that if they weren't interested in
the financing, all they had to do was to let me know in time,
for me to have approached some other institution. For them

to not even have the courtesy to inform me, when at my end I had completed all the formalities and had even kept the margin money aside, was bizarre. When I demanded to speak to their seniors, they simply stopped taking my calls. Interestingly, these were the very people who had made huge bonuses based on our business in Centrum. In fact, they had boasted of their ongoing relationship with Ashneer Grover at Kotak and had tried to win the BharatPe account. Clearly, none of them had any backbone. While they were dealing with people's money, they were treating them shoddily. It wasn't about losing Rs 20 crore of potential profit on this trade, but the fact that these bankers had the audacity to use their core skill of lying with clients across the value spectrum had me agitated.

Exasperated by this highly unprofessional behaviour, I was left with no option but to call my general counsel at BharatPe, Sumeet Singh, to ask him to draft a legal notice to Kotak asking them to either make good the financing or make good the loss that I had incurred on account of their improper handling, especially since they had committed the IPO financing in writing months before and had the documentation completed one day before the IPO opening.

The response to the legal notice that I received from Kotak only went on to reinforce the image that I have of bankers. They conveniently said that there was no commitment from them and covered it up with pure legalese. Hide behind lawyers when confronted with your lies is the typical playbook of bankers, who have mastered the art of taking their clients for granted.

By 1 November, the IPO had closed, and there was no point in pursuing any of this further. What I was sure of, however, was that I was done with my relationship with Kotak Wealth Management due to the manner in which they had treated me; this when I had been a big client for them with a high lifetime value. The matter was thus done and dusted.

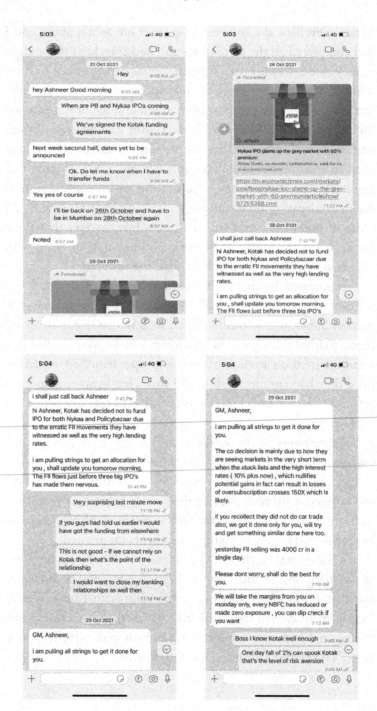

Screen 1 (5:03, 21 Oct 2021)

21 Oct 2021

Hey   8:55 AM

hey Ashneer Good morning   8:55 AM

When are PB and Nykaa IPOs coming   8:56 AM

We've signed the Kotak funding agreements   8:56 AM

Next week second half, dates yet to be announced   8:56 AM

Ok. Do let me know when I have to transfer funds   8:56 AM

Yes yes of course   8:57 AM

I'll be back on 26th October and have to be in Mumbai on 28th October again   8:57 AM

Noted   8:57 AM

26 Oct 2021

Forwarded

Screen 2 (5:03, 26 Oct 2021)

26 Oct 2021

Forwarded

Nykaa IPO glams up the grey market with 80% premium
Abhay Doshi, co-founder, UnlistedArena, said the co...
m.economictimes.com

https://m.economictimes.com/markets/ipos/fpos/nykaa-ipo-glams-up-the-grey-market-with-60-premium/articleshow/87255368.cms   11:22 AM

28 Oct 2021

i shall just call back Ashneer   7:42 PM

hi Ashneer, Kotak has decided not to fund IPO for both Nykaa and Policybazaar due to the erratic FII movements they have witnessed as well as the very high lending rates.

i am pulling strings to get an allocation for you , shall update you tomorrow morning, The FII flows just before three big IPO's

Screen 3 (5:04)

i shall just call back Ashneer   7:42 PM

hi Ashneer, Kotak has decided not to fund IPO for both Nykaa and Policybazaar due to the erratic FII movements they have witnessed as well as the very high lending rates.

i am pulling strings to get an allocation for you , shall update you tomorrow morning, The FII flows just before three big IPO's has made them nervous.   10:46 PM

Very surprising last minute move   11:16 PM

If you guys had told us earlier I would have got the funding from elsewhere   11:16 PM

This is not good - if we cannot rely on Kotak then what's the point of the relationship   11:17 PM

I would want to close my banking relationships as well then   11:18 PM

29 Oct 2021

GM, Ashneer,

i am pulling all strings to get it done for you.

Screen 4 (5:04)

29 Oct 2021

GM, Ashneer,

i am pulling all strings to get it done for you.

The co decision is mainly due to how they are seeing markets in the very short term when the stock lists and the high interest rates (10% plus now) , which nullifies potential gains in fact can result in losses of oversubscription crosses 150X which is likely.

if you recollect they did not do car trade also, we got it done only for you, will try and get something similar done here too.

yesterday FII selling was 4000 cr in a single day.

Please dont worry, shall do the best for you.   7:09 AM

We will take the margins from you on monday only, every NBFC has reduced or made zero exposure , you can dip check if you want   7:12 AM

Boss I know Kotak well enough   9:40 AM

One day fall of 2% can spook Kotak that's the level of risk aversion   9:40 AM

I made another Rs 2 crore in profit on the PolicyBazaar IPO, where I had initially put Rs 8 crore of my own funds, for a Rs 84-crore application, but then I had to wire another Rs 3 crore on the closing day as additional margin money, as the IPO was not as oversubscribed as expected by the financiers. It worked out well for me, with PB opening at almost 25 per cent higher than its IPO price. My participation in the Policy Bazar IPO was through IIFL—the archrival of Kotak Wealth.

When it came to the Paytm IPO, I decided against investing in it. It was sad to see the IPO being overpriced so as to offer a Rs 10,000-crore secondary exit to the Chinese Alibaba group at the cost of the Indian public and Paytm itself, which needed a primary infusion. As a banker, I felt that had Vijay Shekhar Sharma, founder of Paytm, priced the IPO closer to US$16 billion, his stock would still have found support at some level. It has been nothing short of painful to see US$16 billion of its valuation being wiped away and the Paytm stock trading at $6 billion, with other much smaller private fintech firms being valued higher.

26 December 2021

Subject: 'Ashneer at his worst'.

The ping of an email from a rather unusual name caught my attention. From 'Unicon Baba', a name apparently famous on Twitter, the mail was marked to Bhavik and me and contained an audio file some 4 minutes 28 seconds in length, 'allegedly' of me speaking to my relationship manager at Kotak.

Here is how the mail read:

> I will make it public today evening. This is toxic guys, you can't threaten to kill people. WTF!

I, of course, didn't take the mail seriously and replied with:

> Haha – people will manufacture any fiction. I don't think I need to respond to this manufactured audio – fun to hear it though.

Promptly came a reply, asking me to take his threat seriously:

> Boss, you are not understanding the gravity of the situation. Law enforcement agencies will only decide. Once it is out it will be out of my control.

I once again replied to him, explaining the facts clearly:

Dude – please be thoughtful about what you post. The world is after me to disrepute – it's up to you to be their pawn or apply yourself. First of all let me give you facts – I was at the shoot during the Nykaa IPO. Secondly my wife handles these things not me. Thirdly if there was any sanctity to this – the bank would have escalated/taken recourse then itself not waited for me to come on Shark Tank before leaking this outside. On such things please be mindful – don't get played is all I would say. You've to understand I can get financing elsewhere – which I have for subsequent IPOs. Let me send you something which will make you believe all this.

Unicon Baba persisted with his agenda, despite my email and continued with his threats:

'The world is after me to disrepute' – I know this and agree 100% –biggest names and more powerful ones in the industry are waiting for an opportunity. 1.5X to 2X offers for your employees are ready. I am not joking. Your wife is also a party btw as per the court of law. I got this audio 2 months back. But I didn't do anything. Shark Tank just triggered me and that's it. Up to you to decide.

I tried to reason with him yet another time with:

Sir – I've told you what's the truth. I don't think any one of us can comment on fiction. It's up to you sir – here is a clear communication – I was the aggrieved party there and I did not say anything despite the other party clearly lying on WhatsApp – you know Kotak ended up funding both the IPOs. As I said – this audio is ridiculous and doesn't have any legal sanctity and is fake. I did not get the 2X–3X employee offer thing. What's that?

At this point, Bhavik, who was marked on the emails, intervened to ask me if he should speak to Unicon Baba. '*Tu usko jaanta hai* (Do you know him)?' was my surprised reaction, especially since Unicon Baba had somehow chosen to mark Bhavik in the mails. '*Mera connect hai* (I have a connection),' he said. I gave my assent for him to go ahead and see what the matter was.

Bhavik reverted in some time, stating that Unicon Baba was demanding $240,000 as marketing money from us to hush up this audio. Then, Unicon Baba's email promptly arrived.

Hello Team,

As was discussed sharing advertising plans

Unicon Baba Early Stage Investors List Advertiser Rate Card for BharatPe

Ad Unit	Period	Category	Cost	Currency
BharatPe Banner of UB Investor	24 months		Banners on all sheets	
List 240,000 USDT				

Unicon Baba Early Stage Investor List

https://docs.google.com/spreadsheets/d/1apBh9pNKvoLovDoS48QUGCXZhC-6H363uO31M4COIjg/

USDT Address
0x104288958be8e70B9A7a80723174eBDc4561d9Dc

You can expect 800–1000 high potential startup deals in 2 years easily. Also I will help you in image building strategy that will change the narrative. And give 20–25 positive shoutouts and PR plugs in the said period.

Let me know your concerns. Marketing plan shared will absolutely turn around the perception.

Looking for the support thanks.

My response to Unicon Baba, of course, was that, read with his previous email, this was pure blackmail, which I wouldn't succumb to. I went on to add that my relationship manager from Kotak, whom the purported fake audio was accusing me of threatening, was in my office today to exchange New Year pleasantries:

> Hi. Please stop seeking US$240,000 in BITCOINS in exchange for making this fake audio public. This is tantamount to extortion and I am hoping that's not the case here (for the sake of your own credibility on twitter). Please see here Su (the purported other person in your fake audio) in our office yesterday to exchange pleasantries for new year (along with hearty laugh on this fake audio) and agree on joint legal action in case of any misadventures from you here. Also please stop sending these fake audios/memes to our investors – we don't understand your agenda/vendetta. Regards. Ashneer

I attached the photo for good measure to the email and forgot about this rather curious episode.

In early January 2022, I was visiting Udaipur with my parents. This was the time when the early episodes of *Shark Tank* were being aired, and I was surprised to see that people were recognizing me even behind the COVID mask. On waking up one morning I found my phone buzzing with multiple messages. The first one was from Micky Malka. 'There's an audio on Twitter. Is that you?' he asked without much ado or context.

On logging in to Twitter, I saw that some account called @ BabuBongo had put up a SoundCloud link with an audio clip. 'How rich founders treat poor bank employees,' the caption claimed. I thought it was best to nip it in the bud and respond on Twitter itself. I wrote stating clearly that it was a fake audio by some scamster who was trying to extort funds and that I had refused to buckle. I topped this up with a snapshot of the mail I had written to Unicon Baba.

In the meantime, Bhavik intervened to say that he would speak to the Twitter team to get the audio removed. The same evening, the audio was indeed taken down. What I now had up on Twitter was my response to a non-existent audio message. I was advised by my PR person to remove my response now that the original tweet had been taken down. I also went ahead and informed my investors that while I had put out a clear response, it had been taken down simply because the original tweet had been taken down and that there was no value in leaving a comment on a now-removed post. By now, of course, people had put the audio clip on YouTube.

If I thought that, having responded appropriately, controversies were now behind me, I was in for another rude shock. By the time I reached Delhi from Udaipur, there was yet another piece of news doing the rounds. Apparently, now the legal notices exchanged between me and Kotak in early October had been leaked to the media. Only three parties were privy to these legal notices—me, Sumeet Singh (the GC at BharatPe) and Kotak. So the leak was clearly from either my GC or Kotak. With the media teams reaching out to Kotak for their comments, Kotak went ahead and made a statement confirming that the notices had been exchanged and went on to add that I had threatened one of their employees. This unwarranted response from Kotak, which had made no mention of any audio of any kind, gave more fodder to the media. They went ahead and linked it with the audio that had done the rounds earlier and reported that the purported audio must be true.

What was playing out was clearly a well-conspired act, one that took a great toll on me emotionally. Here I was being turned into a villain by the media, when it was me who had been wronged by Kotak and their unscrupulous RMs while I had even given up on them for any recourse. The fact that I was on television at this time made matters worse! People would google me, having seen me on *Shark Tank*, and all they would read is a bunch of negative news around me, further fuelling their hatred.

'Ashneer Grover Case: Kotak Mahindra Bank Pursuing Appropriate Legal Action'—*Business Standard*. 'A Deleted Tweet, an Allegedly Abusive Call: Fintech BharatPe vs Kotak'—NDTV. The headlines rolled non-stop.

'Why are you getting so affected when you haven't done anything?' While my family assured me that with limited attention spans, all of this would blow over, I was in a not-so-great mental space. I decided to lie low and let the news run its course. I even switched off my phone for a few days and let Suhail and Sumeet speak to the investors. The thing that was really bothering me was that all of this couldn't have been a coincidence by any stretch of the imagination and was definitely doctored. Only by whom, I had no idea. Here I had been working hard day in and day out, and ensuring that everyone grew in the process. Someone, however, was clearly working harder and smarter to pull me down and finish me.

'Sequoia has suggested that we hire a new media agency, which is good at crisis management, that could help us get our point of view across,' Bhavik informed me amid this media blitzkrieg. When I didn't see anything appearing in the press that put forth our viewpoint, it left me wondering if the agency was appointed to work for me or against me.

'Are you okay?' Madhuri asked, sensing that there was palpable tension in the air one morning. 'I just got a phone call from Sumeet. He said he had heard from Suhail that, apparently, Uday Kotak was exploring if an FIR could be filed against me,' I informed her, shocked at the bizarre turn this whole incident was taking. If I thought my disclosure would stress her out, it was her question that surprised me instead. 'Are you sure you are being fed the right information internally?' she asked. 'I don't know, Mads. The one thing that you have set me thinking about is that the only person privy to the legal notices was Sumeet, since he was the one who had drafted them. The fact that the story of the legal notices was raked up months after the notices were actually exchanged makes the whole episode quite uncanny. Something sinister is at work. Either way, I have made up my mind. I think the only way to kill this harmful noise is for me to go on voluntary leave for a few days. That should put the gossip mills to rest, and we will be able to focus on our business. There are far too many deliverables,' I said, sharing my plan with Madhuri.

'The media is going berserk, and I haven't seen any media plans from you guys. I am suggesting therefore that I go on leave for a few days so that the issue dies down,' I said to Bhavik, Sumeet and Suhail, whom I had called for a meeting at my house. My brother-in-law, Shonak, was also in the room, though he sat a little away to study the body language of everyone.

'It's not a good idea. We need to weather the storm,' Bhavik immediately rubbished my idea. 'Investors are asking us to have a forensic test conducted to prove that the audio was indeed not Ashneer's.' Suhail and Sumeet seemed to egg me on, only for me to remind them that I did not need to prove anything to anyone. 'I do not think there is any need for you to go on leave. For over three years, investors have only seen good days with us, they should be patient. You can send in a proposal for voluntary leave if you wish, but at the board with the investors we will turn it down, stating that we cannot run the business without you,' Bhavik said, making his intention clear. With my decision made, that I would send in a leave letter, and their decision made, that they would reject it, I set out to pen down my thoughts. 'You can send a draft to my personal ID, for me to have a look and suggest changes if any,' Sumeet offered.

After that meeting, I made a weekend trip to Panipat along with Madhuri to meet my in-laws. While I am not a religious person, on this trip Madhuri took me to meet a Jain *muni* in Chandigarh, shaken as we were at the developments that seemed to have taken us by storm. One look at me and the Jain muni, an English-speaking gentleman, asked me to reflect on two questions: 'Are you happy? Are the people around you pure?' I was left a little shaken at his questions, what with the recent happenings. It was only a matter of time before my answer to both these questions would be an unequivocal 'no'.

Back at Panipat, I received a call from Micky on my son's number, since he'd found mine switched off. 'You know I love you and have been your biggest supporter, but you have to lose this battle to live another day to fight the war my friend!' was his rather strange message that left me thoroughly confused. I confessed to Madhuri and her dad that things didn't seem quite right.

Back home, as per my original plan, I sat down to pen a heartfelt note that spoke of the relentless work I had put in at BharatPe, adding that I was proceeding on a temporary, voluntary leave of absence till the end of March. My note clearly said that I would use this period to 'think deeply about our next phase of product development, and BharatPe's path to profitability and IPO'. While Sumeet did send some comments to Madhuri on my note, I chose not to incorporate them, as I was not writing a legal document but something that my heart told me. Once I had sent the letter formally to the board and the investors, Suhail topped up my letter with a note to the board, stating that this was an overreaction from Ashneer and that a meeting should be called to decide the course of action. A copy of that note was forwarded to Madhuri. I was subsequently filled in by Kewal Handa and others, that an informal board meeting was called on 13 January, which wasn't taken on record, where my leave application was unanimously turned down.

In fact, I went and personally met Rajnish Kumar. Madhuri's NIFT batchmate's dad, Rajnish was a former SBI chairman, whom I had happened to meet earlier that year and who had agreed to join us as a professional director for a sitting fee of Rs 50 lakh a year and ESOPs worth Rs 2 crore. (It is another matter that on his first day in office itself, he arm-twisted me and got the ESOPs revised to Rs 3 crore—an early sign of greed and bad intent that I should have read.) Rajnish was my fourth hiring mistake—the proverbial last nail in my coffin—the other three being Suhail Sameer (CEO), Jasneet (CHRO) and Sumeet Singh (GC).

Rajnish's expressed view at this time also was that the matter had been blown out of proportion by the media and that it would die its own death. He tried to mediate on the issue by speaking to some high-level person in Kotak. Rajnish Kumar is on the Kotak Fund board.

While I thought the issue was drawing to a close, I had no idea of the bloodbath that was to follow.

14

The Ultimate Deception

My exit from BharatPe has been the most publicly covered controversy of the start-up world. Thanks to unscrupulous folks masquerading as media personnel, but more importantly thanks to my own stakeholders, who plotted the most Machiavellian plot to get rid of the creator of the company. In the following pages you will find that the truth is indeed much stranger than fiction. And it's never public.

I need to introduce you to a set of characters, along with their motivations against me, to help you understand the nuances of the plot.

1. Shashvat Mansukhbhai Nakrani: The twenty-year-old co-founder who dropped out of IIT Delhi and made millions by just being in 'the right place at the right time'. He is the epitome of 'doing nothing pays the most'. Influenced by Suhail, the CEO who joined later, Shashvat's invaluable contribution in the plot was that he was a signatory to the SHA and a founder–director, and proved to be a perfect tool for others to use. He has not uttered a word in any board meeting

and not a single penny by any investor was put on him. With me becoming the sole face of BharatPe, he probably started feeling much smaller, and he must have been needled about this by the other plotters. Even after I had ensured that he and his dad made crores in secondaries, he didn't even so much as pick up my call during the whole episode. Ironically, I was the one who had shielded him from my investors while I did the heavy-lifting as he went back to IIT Delhi and completed his graduation, having dropped out of the institute earlier.

2. Bhavik Koladiya: 'Et tu, Brute?' It was most painful for me to discover that he was among the traitors. I was the only person who believed him and led him to attain redemption after his unsuccessful start in the US. I had allowed him to do a secondary of Rs 4 crore within months of starting BharatPe, when the company had raised only Rs 1.9 crore. I had entrusted him with handling tech, his passion. Importantly, I had never treated him as anything less than a brother. Bhavik stayed in my fully furnished house in Malviya Nagar for two years without paying a single penny of rent. Madhuri gave his wife crores as loans for her to start her business. Did he start feeling left out after BharatPe became big? Or did Suhail and Sumeet use their drinking and smoking sessions to slowly poison him against me, despite his good sense telling him not to believe them? Or did Sumeet promise Bhavik a way back on the BharatPe cap table, with Ashneer out?

3. Sequoia: The one organization—or, rather, the one individual that this political organization is—that had the biggest axe to grind against me. A reluctant investor at first, they are the largest shareholder, owning ~19 per cent equity worth more than US$500 million in BharatPe. With the bank licence and with the launch of PostPe, I was taking the sheen away from Shailendra's ten-year-long investment in Pine Labs, which was supposed to go IPO to give Sequoia its biggest payday.

They had the most to benefit by playing out a merger between BharatPe and Pine Labs—something that would have been impossible to achieve with me around.

4. Micky (Ribbit): The smartest fintech investor on the planet. He is a firm believer in the fact that the US funds had invested in BharatPe on the back of his putting in the money. Also, one who truly believes in the bigoted view that all husband–wife duos working together are frauds. Also, at Robinhood, one of Micky's biggest investments in the US, he had seen the Federal Reserve stifle the company when they came down heavily on them for taking deposits. With that background, did he get spooked easily, fearing that the Kotak issue would make the bank licence at BharatPe go away? Or was he just unhappy that I hadn't listened to his hints and soft messages against going on *Shark Tank* and thought it was time to put me in my place?

5. Rajnish Kumar: Ex-chairman of State Bank of India. Invited to the board by Madhuri and me, he had shown enough early signs of wanting control and to make money out of BharatPe, which I ignored to my detriment. Whether it was getting his ESOPs increased from Rs 2 crore to Rs 3 crore on the first day in office, or asking me to get him free membership to the DLF Golf Course when I held a meeting with Centrum at DLF Golf Links, there were enough and more signs. In the well-executed plot, he played me the longest.

6. Suhail Sameer: The one who made me lose faith in storied institutions such as McKinsey and IIM Lucknow. Suhail detested Madhuri because she saw through his nefarious designs early. Along the way, he was also insecure as I had informed him that a new CFO would be joining us soon, which he thought would clip his wings. I gave him more ESOPs than anyone else had been given in Indian start-ups, giving him Rs 11 crore of liquidity within a year, besides

making him the CEO and even a director on the board. His payback, of course, was in the form of a betrayal. Taking advantage of the fact that I do not indulge in alcohol, he would call Bhavik and Shashvat for drinking sessions and poison them against me.

7. Sumeet Singh: Brought in as GC. I believe he loathed Madhuri for not giving him the lifestyle he always desired. Asked the simple question of why the legal costs of handling cases were spiralling ever since he came in as GC, he had vowed, '*Inko toh main dekh loonga* (Now I'll show them their place).' Also, he believed that while he was a lawyer, he was equally capable of doing business. In my estimation, he was a delusional bragger and a backstabber who was jealous of my meteoric rise.

All these people were, as Madhuri rightly referred to them in a letter to the board, male chauvinists. Also, the last three had a very peculiar commonality—all of them had negotiated ESOP terms (vesting in one or two or three years) which were far better than the whole firm. In fact, even as a founder I was subject to a four-year lock-in, but not them.

Let me also lay out a detailed sequence of the plot for you. The plot was played out in six well-synchronized phases.

- Phase I: 6–19 January: Engineer Ashneer out as MD on temporary leave. Take control of the board.
- Phase II: 16–26 January: Bring in lawyers and accountants, and create a pretext for converting his temporary leave to permanent leave.
- Phase III: 26 January–18 February: Do a sham investigation and create pressure on Madhuri and Ashneer to resign by leaking everything to the press.
- Phase IV: 18 February–1 March: Conveniently terminate Madhuri (not protected by SHA), continue with media

leaks and, therefore, create a pretext for removing Ashneer under SHA.

- Phase V: 1 March: The endgame.
- Phase VI: 1 March onwards: Keep putting false information out to the media to defame Ashneer in a public trial.

Phase I: Send Ashneer on Temporary Leave

With information that my voluntary leave had been summarily rejected, I decided it was time to pull myself up and get back to office. I had always been a builder, and stressful times were even more so a reason to focus on what I did best: build. I was, however, in for a rude shock. On messaging Micky Malka on WhatsApp, that I would be in office the following day, in a bizarre turn of events, I was met with the following response:

1. You need your board to support and approve that this is the best path for the company; 2. The company still needs to finish the diligence and investigation which is not yet finalized; 3. A code of conduct needs to be approved; 4. You need to organize a board meeting before you go back to office as the board needs to approve if it's the right decision; 5. The board needs to see a media plan and a regulatory risk assessment of the consequences; 6. A plan needs to be put in place to communicate to the entire team the findings and adjustments. Only after all of this you should be back at work. Is this clear?

This certainly had nothing to do with the Kotak issue at hand. That Micky was at full play was clear for me to see.

18 January 2022, 10.29 p.m.

True to Micky's plan, an invitation to a board meeting, to be conducted at 8 a.m. the next morning, soon hit my mailbox.

19 January 2022, 7.55 a.m.

Micky Malka's name flashing on my phone right before the board meeting had me surprised. 'Hope you are ready. Stay calm during the meeting,' was Micky's uncalled-for advice that set the ground for the fact that the events. about to unfold, would be hostile, to put it mildly.

8 a.m., BharatPe Board Meeting

Having logged in to the Zoom call and with the statutory aspects of the board meeting taken care of, Micky jumped right into the business at hand and said that it would be in the best interests of the company if I were to go on voluntary leave. He then called upon the others to express their views.

To my astonishment, Shashvat, Suhail and Sumeet all endorsed the decision that I was to go on leave.

How could this be true? There had to be a mistake. My mind was racing. After all, these were the very people who had slammed my proposal of going on voluntary leave in the first place and had subsequently informed me that the board had already turned my proposal down in the 13 January meeting. I was in a state of total shock, and my eyes were now scrutinizing the Zoom window that featured Bhavik. 'Why are we sending him on leave? We need him now more than ever.' I heard Bhavik say this. He broke the transfixed state that the events had thrown me into, questioning why I was being sent on leave. I became extremely emotional and asked the board why it was cornering me when they themselves had earlier turned down my proposal of going on a voluntary leave of absence. If I thought my impassioned plea would have an impact, I had underestimated them. The day's shocks clearly weren't over. It was a matter of time before Bhavik made a volte-face in the same meeting and sided with the others, stating that my going on leave wasn't a bad idea after all.

The only two people who were in disagreement with the majority were Rajnish Kumar and Kewal Handa, but they did not have a vote. 'Your own team isn't standing tall with you and is in favour of your going on leave.' Micky Malka's words brought me face to face with the rude fact that I was fighting a lost battle. It was an extremely emotional moment for me, one where I felt totally let down by the very people I had nurtured and shielded.

'Okay, if this is what you all want, I will proceed on voluntary leave. Do you want Madhuri to go as well?' I asked rhetorically, emotions claiming the better of me. At this point, Rajnish Kumar asked me to drop off from the call, enabling them to discuss the matter. I was informed via a phone call a few minutes later that the company had accepted my proposal to proceed on voluntary leave and that I should send the letter formally to the company, and also call for a town hall and convey my decision to all employees.

Still reeling from the shock, given the manner in which this coup was carried out, I asked Madhuri to go to work and see that everything was being executed correctly. In the meantime, I gathered myself enough to arrange for flowers to be sent to all employees with a note that said that it was a tough phase for the company, one that all of us needed to brave through. I went on to assure them that I would be back soon from my voluntary leave. Nothing, however, could have prepared me for the distraught state in which Madhuri returned from work that day. 'I cannot tell you the kind of negative vibes I experienced today,' she said about her ordeal. 'Everyone's body language has changed. Suhail was sitting with his feet up, and I even heard him speaking to journalists.' This when it was expressly discussed that other than issuing a press release for my leave, nobody from the company would interact with the media.

Even as I tried to counsel Madhuri not to take things to heart, the ping of a message on my phone had me fuming. It was a message from Suhail demanding that Madhuri resign. Kewal Handa had apprised me after the board meeting that the proposal for Madhuri to resign was rejected by the board, and that if anyone told me anything to the contrary I should be on guard. I wrote back to Suhail, stating that Madhuri's resignation hadn't been accepted by the board. To which his reply was that Harshjit and Micky wanted Madhuri to go. 'Stay away from the matter' was my unequivocal response to him. Clearly, all of them had new masters now—I was nobody to them already.

Phase II: Let's Make Their Leave Permanent

20 January 2022

The spate of shocking events continued unabated as I received an email suggesting that the minutes of the board meeting record that I had made a request for voluntary leave, which the board had accepted. It went on to mention that Madhuri's resignation had also been accepted.

I couldn't believe that they could all act in concert and stoop so low. I wrote back immediately, stating that not only did I know that the board hadn't accepted Madhuri's resignation, technically, I couldn't render the resignation on her behalf when she herself had not been present in the meeting. Clearly, an emotional call by me in the meeting was being used to their advantage. On my dissent, the minutes were rectified.

Madhuri decided not to go to work the next morning, given the massacre that was playing out. The office, I was told later by people who were in attendance, was buzzing with activity that day, only not of the positive kind that we had become used to seeing over the last three and a half years.

Usually, my father is a passive participant in my business discussions. That day, however, he expressed strong resentment with respect to Suhail and Sumeet's betrayal. While Madhuri had, on several occasions, expressed her reservations to me about these people, I had thought she was being a little too sceptical. To hear my father say the same thing that day rang a loud bell, making me realize how a conspiracy had been planned under my nose.

I decided to write to the board asking how Bhavik, who was neither an employee nor a shareholder, had taken over the systems in office. I asked pointedly if this was the reason they were insisting that I go on leave. Not one person chose to reply to my mail. What we got instead was a mail from Suhail to Madhuri, stating that she had been put on temporary leave pending investigation on corporate governance matters, and hence her entry to office was also barred.

Interestingly, I heard from Bhavik at this point, who suggested that we should meet. With the meeting fixed at the Panchshila Club, he came in at the appointed hour to tell me, '*Mujhe nahi pata kya ho raha hai aur ise kaise khatam karna hai. Suhail kuch chala raha hai* (I don't know what is transpiring. It is all Suhail's doing).' I don't think I had the ability to empathize with him at that point, except to remind him that he was the one who had turned against me in the board meeting. While my guess was that he had only come to me to fish for some information on what my next move would be, I decided to play along with him. I told him categorically that if he indeed wanted to do something, he should meet me along with Shashvat, as we could then jointly remove Suhail from the board. While he agreed to the plan, no marks for guessing that he went cold turkey after this meeting.

22 January 2022

The day began with yet another email. It was suggested that a two-member corporate governance committee comprising, lo and behold, Suhail Sameer and Sumeet Singh, be constituted. While everyone was quick to give their consent on email, I expressed my dissent on the constitution of the committee. The manner of the approval of the resolution was objected to by Rajnish Kumar as well—he expressly mentioned that such approvals could only be sought via discussions during a board meeting. Swiftly after that, an amended circular resolution, dated 23 January, was circulated, appointing Rajnish Kumar to oversee the operation of the review committee. This was when he turned against me. It was also stated that the law firm Shardul Amarchand Mangaldas, where Sumeet Singh was a partner previously, would be appointed as legal adviser to work along with the review committee on the governance review.

I put on the record my disagreement in regard to the composition of the committee, stating that it was against the shareholders' agreement as well as the articles of association, which requires committees of the board to have the same composition as the board. Sumeet Singh wasn't a board member, and his being on the review committee, therefore, wasn't kosher. My objections, however, were summarily dismissed.

The events that had transpired over the past few days didn't sit well with me, to say the least. The more I thought about them, the more I realized how the planned leaks of the legal notices exchanged with Kotak was an internal task, carried on by Sumeet Singh, who was the only one privy to it, and how it had been used strategically to create a narrative in the media. However, that too had served a limited purpose, and there was an overriding attempt to give a more dramatic spin to the entire episode, what with the setting up of an extremely biased corporate governance committee. I knew for a fact that while I may have been ridiculously busy—in trying to put the bricks of the business in place—to have paid attention to this coup that had brewed right under my nose, I couldn't give up this easily. So I decided to write to the board, that

I was now in a much better place, especially as I had reached out to the Kotak lawyers. I went on to state that while their response didn't amount to a resolution of the issue, it didn't indicate any escalation of the issue. I was now ready to end my voluntary leave and resume office the next day. Within an hour of sending this email, I was invited for yet another board meeting.

25 January 2022

This time when I logged in to the Zoom meeting, one of its windows was occupied by a top lawyer. It would be an understatement to say that his presence in a regular board meeting was extremely strange, but then, everything that was happening was unusual anyway. After 10–15 minutes, Rajnish Kumar joined the meeting; he mentioned that we didn't need the lawyer's presence in the meeting and that he could drop off. Rightly so, as according to them, the lawyer's presence had achieved the purpose of intimidating me, now that it had been made clear that they had hotshot lawyers to further their agenda. Micky Malka, in the meantime, had pronounced his decision to not switch on his camera during the board meeting. This was probably because he needed to continuously WhatsApp the other attendees, in case they weren't toeing the line. Clearly, the oath that we began every board meeting with, one that confirmed that there wasn't anyone else in the room with us (who could impact our decision-making), had no meaning if we were being given regular instructions on the phone. If only the company would put out videos of these board meetings or the ROC would ask for a record of them, it would be clear that Indian companies had become puppets at the hands of foreign investors.

While I had put on record my dissent on the review committee not complying with the shareholders' agreement as well as the articles of association of the company, I once again raised an objection in the board meeting. Sumeet was not even on the board and couldn't be a part of any committee. And if the review had anything to do with the Kotak issue, Sumeet was the one who was, in fact, instrumental in drafting the legal notice to Kotak. So how could he be sitting on judgement in a matter in which he was involved? On the issue of Suhail's appointment to the committee, too, I pointed out that Suhail didn't have a board seat by virtue of having become the CEO. While Shashvat and I had nominated him to the board, I now wanted to withdraw the nomination. As for the appointment of Amarchand Mangaldas & Co., my submission to the board was that the said company wasn't an impartial establishment. Sumeet Singh was an ex-Amarchand employee. '*Shardul mujhe apna beta samajhta hai. Sahib mujhe apni kothi pe bulate hai weekend pe* (Shardul thinks of me as his son),' Sumeet himself had bragged to me. But all my arguments fell on deaf ears, as in their minds they had already written my obituary.

Interestingly, for the first time on 25 January, the engagement of Alvarez & Marsal, a management consulting firm, was brought up before the board. It felt as if I was in a time warp, as I was now being told that this firm, which had just been appointed apparently, had even come up with some preliminary findings, basis which I was being put on a compulsory leave of absence. That the report of Alvarez & Marsal was dated as early as 24 January was something that I would learn from media reports later. Had they, therefore, issued the report even prior to their official engagement?

Shocked beyond belief at the inexplicable events that were playing out, I raised several other questions in the board meeting. What had led them to initiate the entire process in the first place? If corporate governance was a generic review of companywide policies, as the communication seemed to suggest, why wasn't everyone under its ambit and why weren't they being sent on leave? None of which met with any reply; instead, I was unceremoniously asked to drop off the call, for the board to put the proposal to vote.

A mail from Rajnish Kumar the following day stated that the board had resolved that I should proceed on a compulsory leave of absence and that I wasn't allowed to speak to anyone associated with the company other than to him.

Phase III: The Media Blitzkrieg

Now it was time for Sequoia to flex their muscles. While I had been instructed to maintain confidentiality, every single minute of the board meeting was being fed to the press, real time, as were alleged findings from predetermined reports, which were yet to be presented to the company or the board.

In fact, each time that reports were leaked to the media, I would write to Rajnish Kumar asking him why he was allowing this to happen. 'It is a big, leaky organization. I've instructed everyone to give me things in sealed envelopes and not on email,' he told me, which was a lame defence, in my opinion.

In the meantime, a full-fledged and funded campaign was underway in the media, aimed at maligning my image. Each report had company executives 'requesting anonymity' and feeding malicious rumours. A report in Livemint said that BharatPe was likely to sack Ashneer Grover amid 'fraud concerns'. The same report went on to state that the services of Madhuri had been terminated. 'Jain helmed procurement, finance and human resources from the company's early days. She is a graduate of the National Institute of Fashion Technology, and she was running a fashion boutique before joining BharatPe . . . At times, the company did try to look at hiring a qualified CFO (chief financial officer), but Grover turned down that decision,' went the rather spiteful and false report. The fact of the matter was that in October itself, I had convinced a highly regarded IIT Delhi–IIM Calcutta alum to join us as CFO, whose offer letter had been issued by Suhail Sameer himself. Of course, for good measure, Suhail Sameer went on record saying, 'BharatPe was urging the media not to speculate in advance of the report and make a judgment based on uninformed sources.'

As late as 9 February, I got to know that PwC had also been appointed to assist the review committee. This afterthought was clearly because the SHA says that a founder can be terminated for 'gross negligence or willful misconduct' only when such conduct is determined by a 'Big 4 firm that doesn't have any relation with the company'. To tick this box and fulfil this clause, PwC had now been appointed in haste. What they had conveniently overlooked was the fact that PwC had a long association with the company, as it had worked with BharatPe on several occasions. Interestingly, Sequoia's CFO, Harshal Kamdar, who had put into place Bhavik's exit from the cap table and later joined Sequoia, was also an ex-PwC employee. Such facts couldn't deter them, as this clearly was a fait accompli, and, I suspect, the review committee was set up with the motive of terminating my appointment in the first place.

As for the much-hyped Alvarez & Marsal report, the media, of course, was privy to it even before it was presented to the board. 'Financial Irregularities Found at BharatPe; Followed Process Says Company', *Hindu BusinessLine*, 4 February 2022. 'Missing Consultants, Dubious Payments, Nonexistent Vendors: What the BharatPe Probe Revealed', Moneycontrol.com, 4 February 2022. Enough and more media headlines quoted the elusive A&M report that hadn't made its way to a board meeting or to the people who were being accused of a host of wrongdoings by it.

Madhuri, in fact, wrote a letter to Alvarez & Marsal asking them how this report had allegedly 'leaked'. 'Even assuming that such a report does exist, it is common practice that where there is a report making allegations against or casting aspersions against any individual, the identity of such an individual is kept confidential,' she went on to ask, only to be met with a deafening silence. Clearly, the board had taken a blasé position. Given the fact that I was a public figure now, they wanted to go after me in public, and the media was turning out to be a willing cohort.

Madhuri also wrote a scathing mail to the board mentioning, among other things, that since the 'leaked' report alleged several transgressions by her, she would step down only when she had cleared her name. That, of course, was an opportunity that wasn't accorded to her, as the next set of events had already started to roll.

15

Truth Is Stranger than Fiction

Phase IV: Let's Get the 'Bitch' First

'You are requested to be available tomorrow at the office of Shardul Amarchand Mangaldas & Co,' read an email from BharatPe to Madhuri one morning.

Our son, Avyukt, was having his term exams at the time. Madhuri therefore replied to the mail stating that meeting the next day wasn't convenient for her; she even went on to attach the exam schedule of the Shri Ram School while requesting for time the following week. In her email, she also mentioned her discomfort at meeting at a lawyer's office, as the choice of venue itself amounted to an act of intimidation. The response to the email was far from amicable. The mail categorically said that this was an act of non-compliance on her part and that while the meeting was now being rescheduled for the day after at the Imperial Hotel, failure to appear at the said date would amount to termination of her services.

By this time, I had realized that this was likely to turn into a legal battle and that I had to lawyer up. I had, therefore, approached a lawyer named Siddharth Bhavnani, who had worked as the general counsel at Grofers and later set up his own law firm. We had great respect for each other professionally. So much so that when I was setting up BharatPe, Siddharth had gone on to invest a small amount in the company while also helping us create the company's SHA. 'I am happy to work with you and to recuse myself of all mandates at BharatPe,' was his immediate response when I approached him. BharatPe, however, refused to give him an NOC and went on to withhold all payments due to him for work he had done for the company. Sumeet was at play here, of course, since he was responsible for clearing those bills now.

Through my brother-in-law, advocate Shonak Sharma, I was then led to Raian Karanjawala, a well-known lawyer of repute, whose daughter had gone to law school with Shonak. On meeting him at the office of Karanjawala & Co. in New Friends Colony in Delhi, I recounted the entire sequence of events to him, showing how I had been set up big time. 'I was on a mission to create value and didn't have time for such politics,' I offered by way of explanation, which made me sick as I spoke.

While he gave his assent to take up the mandate immediately, he needed to seek an NOC from PhonePe, as Karanjawala had worked with them on certain trademark-related issues. The NOC sought, I was put in touch with his team—on the civil side, Ruby Ahuja; and on the criminal side, Sandeep Kapoor, who had shot into the public eye lately, having obtained the elusive bail in the Aryan Khan case.

When the mail was received summoning Madhuri for a meeting, Sandeep Kapoor offered to accompany her. I recall driving Madhuri down to the Imperial Hotel in my Porsche and walking her till the door of the meeting room, where I was greeted by the lawyers and the accounting folks. I, of course, waited outside the meeting venue. While Madhuri informed them that this being a legal matter, she would like her lawyer, Sandeep Kapoor, to be in attendance, this wasn't acceptable to them. Given their objection, Sandeep Kapoor, a fiery lawyer who is much like me, desi and solid, and doesn't get intimidated by anyone, promptly laid down some ground rules for the meeting. He stated in unequivocal terms that nothing that transpired in that meeting could be recorded and that a copy of any document that was shown to his client should be made available to him. He also categorically told them that should his client decide to assert her right to not respond to any issue immediately and seek time to respond, it would not be deemed as non-cooperation. After this discussion, all of them stepped out of the room. Unaware of these developments, as I waited outside, the sudden flurry of activity took me by surprise—were we done in fifteen minutes? I was, however, given to understand that they had stepped out to keep their phones in the other room so that no recordings could be made.

The next three hours were spent trying to grill Madhuri, without a minute's break. While not a single piece of paper was presented to her, she was asked questions related to certain day-to-day commercial decisions that were taken in the interest of running the business. 'The questions were inane. They asked me stuff like, "Why did you appoint a certain vendor?" While I tried to explain the process of appointing a vendor, I was riled at a point and even asked them how the BharatPe board appointed SAM and A&M. Did the board take competing quotes?' Madhuri shared her exasperation with me after stepping out. The meeting and the so-called fair hearing was clearly a sham, in which no issue that would later be raised against her was discussed, for fear of the fact that she may provide a reasonable answer to their allegations. Madhuri recounted her interaction, asking some rhetorical questions in the bargain. '*Tujhe pata hai kya hoga* (You know what will happen),' was my response to her after hearing the entire episode and knowing instinctively that the meeting was only a charade.

'BharatPe Sacks Madhuri Jain on Funds Misuse Charge; Cancels Her ESOPs.' Thus ran the headlines on every single media platform the very next morning. Interestingly, the termination letter was received by her a day after the media broke this story. No marks for guessing that none of the allegations against her mentioned in the termination letter had been raised in the meeting.

For the first time I saw Madhuri break down. She had held her own ever since BharatPe had stirred up this controversy. This mala fide personal campaign that was targeted at her, however, broke her spirit. What hit her the hardest was that the company had stooped to a level where they had pulled out a dermatologist bill from her office drawer, which she had paid personally, to build a false narrative against her of misusing company funds for 'beauty treatments'. So deep was her hurt that she wrote to the board that she would agree to all the charges if they could only prove that the company had reimbursed this bill or if she had even presented this bill to the company for reimbursement. Of course, there was no response. The very people who were claiming to be high priests of corporate governance were simply using hired agencies as stamping entities, to further their ulterior motives.

Interestingly, on the day that Madhuri's termination letter was sent, my dad, Madhuri and me were out for some personal work, and Madhuri hadn't checked her email. While we were in the car, I received a call from Bhavik. Extremely sceptical of their motives, Madhuri asked me to put the recorder on as I took the call. 'I am calling from Rajnish Kumar's house,' Bhavik began the conversation, and I could also hear Rajnish in the background. Seeking a meeting, Bhavik asked me if I could come to Rajnish Kumar's house in Ambience Island. Not too keen to do that, I asked Bhavik to meet me at the Panchshila Club instead, to which he replied that he would confer with Rajnish Kumar and get back. *Ye log tujhe phasana chahte hai, inse milne ka ab koi matlab nahi hai* (They want to enrage you to embroil you in another controversy, there is no point meeting them now).' This was my dad and Madhuri's unanimous view as I finished the call.

Before Madhuri's meeting with the lawyers, Rajnish Kumar had already requested for a meeting with me. He met me at the Leela Hotel and told me that he didn't think that I could come back. 'You should take your shares and go,' he had suggested. 'Whether I go or stay is my prerogative. You asked me for the meeting. What do you want?' I had retorted, partly amused. He had then suggested that we put a commercial proposal together for me to leave. Having discussed and typed the proposal on his phone, he wanted me to have a look at it before he sent it ahead. On holding his phone, I saw that the proposal was being sent to Harshjit Sethi of Sequoia. Clearly, he was taking instructions from his new masters—the investors. Nothing, of course, came of the proposal. I knew that another meeting had little meaning.

Bhavik called back in a bit to say that they were willing to meet me at the Panchshila Club. I asked him the agenda. '*Baat karni hai* (We want to speak with you),' was his response, to which I replied, '*Press mein baatein ho toh rahi hai* (The press is replete with talks).' At this point, Bhavik's tone changed completely: '*Tujhe baat nahi karni? Ab tu dekh main teri kaise maarta hoon b*h*nch*d* (You do not want to speak? Wait and watch what I do now),' went his threat. It was when we subsequently checked the mail that we realized that Madhuri's termination letter had just been sent before the call came. Perhaps Bhavik's call was to get a reaction from me on that or to build more pressure on me now that they had achieved the first target.

On conferring with our lawyer, Sandeep Kapoor, we were advised that this was a clear case of a death threat and that we should file a police complaint. 'Please have a complaint drafted and also ask your office to take an appointment at the Hauz Khas police station,' I instructed him. Madhuri, however, thought otherwise. '*Humein police complaint nahi karni* (We don't want to file a police complaint). We can't fall to their level; we have to maintain our dignity in these trying times. Rajnish is my batchmate Prerna's dad after all,' she said. While I went with Madhuri's judgement, I did send the complaint that we had drafted to Rajnish Kumar on WhatsApp with a note—it was only because of Madhuri's regard for him that this complaint was on his phone and not in the case diaries of the Hauz Khas police station. Clearly, the very person whom they had destroyed had saved him. His lament of a reply: *'Tumne mujhe yaha phasa diya. Main toh SBI jaisi organization ka chairman hua karta tha* (You are the one who embroiled me in this madness. I used to be the chairman of an organization like the SBI).' Post this interaction, Rajnish was jittery as he emailed me saying that Suhail, Bhavik and Shashvat were at his place that day to discuss the future strategy of the business.

Phase V: The Endgame

Emergency Arbitration

All through this time, I had maintained a dignified silence and not made any official statement. I had been advised by my legal team to apply for an emergency arbitration with the Singapore International Arbitration Centre (SIAC) as a last, fighting chance. My choices, clearly, were to either wait for BharatPe to release the premeditated corporate governance report and terminate my services, and then keep fighting for years for justice, or to try to seek emergency relief. No matter how slim the chances, I decided to go with the latter option.

My appeal to the SIAC clearly stated that the conduct of the board—right from constituting the review committee to relying upon the preliminary findings of Alvarez & Marsal, which were out after a day's investigation, forcing me to proceed on voluntary leave, putting me on a compulsory leave of absence, the ongoing media leaks—all clearly spoke of their malintent and that it was a clear case of fait accompli.

Interestingly, another half-hearted attempt at a settlement came a day before the scheduled arbitration, when Sequoia reached out to Karanjawala & Co., asking me to meet the AZB team in Mumbai. With the arbitration scheduled for the very next day, I realized that this could be an attempt on their part to derail the events, and hence I deferred the meet to the following week.

17 February 2022

The day-long arbitration process ensued. The board came all guns blazing, with senior lawyers to defend them. From my side, I had appointed senior advocate Darius Khambata to fight my case. We were not granted any immediate emergency relief, even though I was free to take the case to the arbitration tribunal, for it to be heard fully on its merit.

I have to admit that I was extremely distraught. The arbitration tribunal would certainly take time to be set up, while the board could now proceed with its plan in the days to follow. Here I was spending time, energy and money fighting against my own money—one that I had raised for the company that I had painstakingly built against all odds. In that one moment, I decided that I had had enough and that I would resign and not give these losers the pleasure of removing me.

26 February 2022

I write this with a heavy heart as today, I am being forced to bid adieu to a company of which I am a founder. I say with my head held high that today, this company stands as a leader in the fintech world. Since the beginning of 2022, unfortunately, I've been embroiled in baseless and targeted attacks on me and my family by a few individuals who are ready not only to harm me and my reputation but also to harm the reputation of the company, which, ostensibly, they are trying to protect.

From being celebrated as the face of Indian entrepreneurship and an inspiration to Indian youths looking to build their own businesses, I am now wasting myself fighting a long, lonely battle against my own investors and management. Unfortunately, in this battle, the management has lost what is actually at stake—BharatPe.

I had finally carried out the heartrending task of penning my resignation from the company. I poured my heart out in the letter, to say that I had nurtured BharatPe as my baby, while the investors were far removed from the sweat that went into making BharatPe what it was. I pointed out that the investors treated founders as slaves, cutting them as per will. And here I was, the rebel slave, who had to be hanged in full public view so that nobody else could dare to be like me. I, however, dared them to take away the fact that BharatPe was what it was today because of me, and also the fact that I would continue to be the single largest individual shareholder of the company.

'So when do we end this, we end this now,' ended my resignation letter.

Clearly, these last four words were among the toughest that I had put down in my life. But I knew I couldn't participate in this charade any more.

Having got this off my chest, I kept the letter ready to be sent out, on 1 March, knowing that one lot of my restricted shares would come through at the end of the month, something that I had full right to. I was not going to get financially played by anyone now, especially since I had already paid the highest price any founder could have paid for his equity.

28 February 2022, 10 p.m.

Kewal Handa's name flashed on my phone. 'Did these people reach out to you for a settlement?' he began without much ado. By that time, I had lost patience for their cat-and-mouse game. Post the arbitration, they had once again fixed a meeting, this time to be held in Mumbai, but had cancelled it at 11 p.m. the night before. 'All of you are taking me for a ride. While you offer me the carrot of settlement, you crucify me in public. If you can drive a public narrative, so can I. Wait till tomorrow,' I lambasted Kewal Handa, filled with annoyance at the joke they had turned the entire process into.

11.36 p.m.

A calendar invite for a short-notice board meeting hit my mailbox the following morning. In fact, they were in such a hurry to send it that it wasn't accompanied by any agenda. By now I had totally understood their game and the mockery they had turned these board meetings into. Every single person had sold their soul, albeit at different price points. Clearly, my conversation with Kewal Handa had set the stage for this board meeting.

As I had surmised, my removal based on the final report of PwC was tabled before the board. The agenda followed at 11.55 p.m. and stated, 'Tabling of final report of PWC on removal of Ashneer Grover'. It is interesting how, till that point, the board had levelled no allegations against me, and I hadn't been offered any chance to defend myself.

12.03 a.m.

I hit the send button on the resignation letter that I had kept ready while also sending out a copy of my resignation to the press.

My long, lonely battle of the last few months, up to finally being driven to resign from the company I had founded, had been numbing, to say the least. Ever since the malicious campaign had rolled, *aansoo nikalne bhi band ho gaye the*, I had died many deaths in the interim. Having made the decision to quit, however, and having sent the mail, the only emotion I felt was, *ab ise main yahaan khatam karta hoon*, let this episode be behind me. There is a burden that a founder carries with himself. But everything has a value, and this vilification had been stretched too far. More than anything else, I didn't want my family to come under undue mental stress due to this hateful campaign that was running against me.

When I told my family about my resignation, there was a deathly silence all around. Shonak, my brother-in-law, who had seen the drama unfolding blow by blow, broke down. I didn't, however, have the mental space even to grieve. All I wanted to do was crash in my bed and sleep.

The next morning, 1 March, I did two interviews. One with Samidha Sharma and Tarush Bhalla on ET Now, and the other one with Shereen Bhan on CNBC-TV18. One needs to watch these interviews, especially the one with Shereen Bhan, where she can be seen straining to hear what was being said in her earpiece. '*Chalo*, someone also makes money on another's *maiyat*,' I told myself. I left an open challenge for a TV interview with any of my investors or Rajnish Kumar or any other board member. Of course, I haven't heard from any of them about whether they are up for this challenge.

Phase VI: Vilification and Media Trial

On 2 March, news arrived of a board meeting having been held late in the evening of 1 March, where my resignation was accepted. If I thought that having got me out of the way without any bloodshed, the board would keep some of its dignity intact, that was not to be. The official statement from the company read that minutes after I received intimation that an inquiry report would be tabled, I had 'shirked responsibility' and that 'Grover and his family members had engaged in extensive misappropriation of funds and siphoned money away from the company's accounts to lead a lavish lifestyle'. This was as personal as they could have got, this time dragging my family, who had nothing to do with the business, into their vilification campaign.

My early reaction was of total incredulity at what had transpired, followed, in turn, by anger and grief at their reprehensible actions. To come to terms with this deep betrayal wasn't going to be easy. While a part of me didn't even want to spend the emotional energy to counter their shameful narrative, I did muster up the strength to put my story out, now that I didn't have a gag order on me. A LinkedIn post that I put up asked some very basic questions, the first of them being: Who among Amarchand, PwC and A&M had started doing audits on 'lavishness' of lifestyle? Had the investors themselves forgotten that they had bought shares from me in Series C, D and E? I even put out a picture of my fundraising trip to the US, where I was raising the $370-million Series E round and had no qualms about sleeping on the floor, invited by friends with open hearts to their homes. I decided to put it out there that the only thing lavish about me were my dreams and my ability to achieve them against all odds, through hard work and enterprise. Importantly, I hoped that the board would get back to work since I, as a shareholder, was worried about the value destruction that was now on a free run.

That single LinkedIn post was read by over 6.2 million people! That told me that, irrespective of the company narrative, people were willing to listen to the truth, and that anyone who would stop by to ask five basic questions could pull down the flimsy version of the story that the company had built in the media.

Of course, as a retaliation to this post, many other stories were floated to the press by the board as a testament to my extravagant lifestyle. 'He also bought a Porsche,' claimed an undisclosed source in yet another story. My limited response to that was that as long as the source of funds for the car was legitimate and came through the investors buying my shares, what was so great about owning a second-hand luxury car? The masterstroke, of course, was the story of the alleged Rs 10-crore dining table, which deserves to be told in some detail for its sheer ingenuity.

The Rs 10-Crore Dining Table

Of the many things for which I have been written about, I didn't think a dining table would ever make the cut. Yet a Rs 10-crore dining table is what many people have come to know me for. I don't think that I would ever want to hold a place in the *Guinness Book of World Records* for owning the most expensive table in the world.

The dining table story is a classic example of malintent on the one hand, and, on the other, of how the media laps up unverified stories and adds liberal doses of masala to them. Sample this:

'A ₹1 crore dining table? How startup king Ashneer Grover lost his luster'—Livemint, 11 March 2022

'होश उड़ा देगी अशनीर ग्रोवर की रईसी: भारत-पे के कर्मचारियों ने खोले राज, डाइनिंग टेबल-पोर्श पर खर्च किए दस करोड़ रुपये'—*Amar Ujala*, 12 March 2022

That's a 10x increase from a mainstream English daily to a more mass-based Hindi publication. Hail the press!

Now to the real story, which is as bizarre as it can get. Madhuri and I had bought the said dining table when we were setting up our new home in Panchsheel Park in Delhi in 2021. A stone table, it was rather heavy. Over one of our conversations at a dinner I had hosted for my then colleagues at BharatPe, I had mentioned how we had to get a pulley to lift this rather *bhaari* (heavy) table into our house; the table weighed as much as 150 kilograms. Little did I know then that creative storytelling would reach quite another level in the near future. In the desire to provide the media with fodder on my 'lavish' lifestyle, the 'bhaari' was translated as being super expensive and the 150 kilos was turned into it $150,000. An ode perhaps to several funding rounds where I'd raised millions of dollars for the company!

A knowledgeable journalist then used a reasonable exchange rate of Rs 70 to a dollar and turned it into a Rs 1-crore dining table. Someone else perhaps inadvertently added a zero or possibly did it in a bid to make my lifestyle seem even more extravagant, and its value was pegged at Rs 10 crore. Thus unfolded this crazy saga that had both mainstream and social media in a tizzy for days.

If I find a buyer for the table at Rs 10 crore, I will be happy to have an exit with an over 200x payout. While the real table that I have is still expensive in my opinion, at Rs 5 lakh, the memes that it has since then inspired are, indeed, priceless! On a more serious note, I would rather put Rs 10 crore in business and create employment for thousands of folks, so that they can earn and put a dignified meal on the table for their families. I have made my way up from a middle-class background, and that's how my brain is trained to think.

I continue to own 8.43 per cent equity in BharatPe, worth $240 million, and am the single largest individual shareholder.

Epilogue

There you are, with that crazy real-life tale of Ashneer Grover, you have heard it all. It's a story that has had its share of heroes, villains, character artists and more. A lived story, one which has left me with a lot more experience, a lot more grey hair, a lot more insight into who my actual friends and well-wishers are; a lot more understanding of 'doglapan'—of success in failure and failure in success; a deeper understanding of what in life really matters; and, needless to mention, it has given me enough opportunities to embrace with equanimity the many curveballs that life throws. My lifespan also happened to overlap with the growth of the tech ecosystem in India, and, inadvertently, I saw myself become the public face of entrepreneurship in the country.

But what is it that I really want to leave you with? Is it for you to think that I was a victim of circumstances? Do I want you to view me as a superhero, having pulled things along this far? Far from it. What, then, is my idea of taking you through this roller coaster of events? After all, things that transpired in my past are of no consequence to you. If there could be anything of consequence, it is how my story can add value to your life and how it can impact your future. And that is something I owe to you, since you have spent money on this book, which you could very well have spent gorging on a pizza or relaxing with a few pints of beer. Not to mention the fact that you have also invested several hours reading these fifteen chapters full of high drama. So as a tailpiece, I would like to share with you what in my opinion worked for my thundering success and led to my catastrophic failure. For, clearly, there are elements of both in my story—just like crests and troughs of waves. If my learnings can make a difference to your life story, I'd consider the effort I put into sharing my journey with you worthwhile.

So here goes: the five things which propelled me towards success and the five failings that pulled the rug from under me. In true social-media style, I present to you a listicle.

1. Fire in Your Belly

My first mantra of success, clichéd as it may sound, is to have a strong fire in your belly. Growing up in a middle-class household, I always had the *bhookh*, the hunger, the unflinching desire to resurrect what my grandparents had lost as migrants and to rise in life. While I didn't come from abject poverty, there was always a gap between my aspirations and the means. In hindsight, this was what motivated me to work towards the life of my dreams. The more you are ensconced in your comfort zone, the less motivated you feel to achieve something. As I see it today, this 'bhookh' is not so prevalent in the metros. It is in the tier-2 and -3 towns, in the Kendriya Vidyalaya and the government school kids that one sees this desire to rise and to turn around one's life for generations to come. Of course, you are more than welcome to prove me wrong; you will only be better off doing it!

2. *Naukri Karke Koi Raees Nahi Bana* (A Job Cannot Make You Rich)

First things first, I am not anti-naukri. After all, I have spent nine years in naukri myself. My mom has been a government school teacher and my dad ran his CA practice; so it is not as if I come from a business family that looks down upon those who do a nine-to-five job. It is just that my experience tells me that while with a job you can just about beat the rate of inflation and maintain your lifestyle, you can't really hope to 'live it up'. With many of you in jobs, this learning may not go down very well with you, but the fact remains that if you want to look at building a better lifestyle, the lure of a 'regular income' is what you will need to forgo. As a businessman, you have to have the patience and the appetite to not live by a monthly paycheck; instead, you have to know that you might get a huge windfall perhaps only once a year, which will be far more than what a naukri-wala can ever imagine.

3. 'Rees', or the Innate Desire to Live the Life of Someone More Successful and Be in Their Shoes

The common advice that we give our children is not to spend time with people who have more money than us, for fear that the child may develop a complex or will get spoilt—*bigad jaayega*. I have a contrarian view. In fact, it is important to spend time with people who have done better in life than us. That is the only way you will know what you need to aspire towards and what that life is. The next time someone who is financially well-to-do invites you to their house, go there by all means. Observe and aspire. If you do feel small, it is that feeling that might ignite the fire in you to do something. *Andar se ek awaaz aa jayegi ki mujhe bhi ye kar ke dikhana hai*— an inner voice will tell you that I need to achieve it too. '*Agar iske paas yeh sab kuchh hai to mere paas kyun nahi* (Why not me)?'

4. Delegate, Delegate, Delegate

The thumb rule of the game is that *akele koi kuch nahi ukhaad sakta*, you simply cannot be a one-man army. While you need people, as a founder you have to be able to delegate work to people so that you can focus on the bigger picture. It may sound easy but is actually one of the most difficult transitions to make—the shift from doing to leading. More so since in our education system we are continuously taught self-reliance, that we need to work hard ourselves, that we need to upskill ourselves, and more. But we are never taught that we also need to get the best out of other people. While it is good to know how to do things yourself, as a leader it's not your job to do them: you have teams for that labour. While I don't code, I can create that buzz among techies and get them to work for me by giving them BMW bikes!

5. Don't Be Transactional

If investors have been willing to put as much as $625 million on my ability to scale a business, a large part of this success has been because I have never been transactional in my approach. I never think of a person in terms of what he can do for me in that transaction. When I was raising a Series D round, for example, I didn't hesitate from speaking to people who had refused to participate in the Series A. The whole world is connected, so to think what you will achieve by speaking to a certain someone at that point in time is short-sighted thinking. As a founder, you have to live your story and share it with as many people as possible—it doesn't matter if he is a peon, CEO of a company, competition, investor or the regulator. That's how your story will propagate exponentially. It is important to remember that collaboration is the cornerstone of human progress, and transactional relationships can only get you so far.

* * *

Now to the tougher part: the learnings from my failings as a founder! If I think back, it is perhaps these failings that led to my being cut short in my path; they are the reason I have this feeling of unfinished business. So, here is a list of five things that, in my experience, you shouldn't do, or, at the very least, do differently.

1. Don't Forget, as a Founder, That the Game Is between You and Your Customer Alone

The brass tacks of running a business are linked to the understanding that the only two important players are your customer and you. Period. You offer a product or a solution to the customer, and the customer is paying you for it. Everyone else—and that includes your co-founder, your employees, your investors, the regulator, third-party vendors, competition—come between you and your customer in some form. Each of them will, of course, take a piece of your earnings, even before anything comes to you. Before jumping into business, therefore, you have to answer many questions for yourself: Are you okay carrying them along? Are you ready for all of them to take a piece? Are you excited enough by what is left after they have taken their piece and by the overall uncertainty?

While everybody else plays a role in the journey, the real story no doubt lies between you and your customer alone. If you want to run a successful business, *iss baat ko gaanth bandhna hoga*, you will need to write this in stone.

2. The Investor Isn't above You, nor Is He a Validation

In a legacy business, the founder's KPI (key performance indicator) is profit and their 'aukaat', their standing among peer businessmen, depends on the quantum of profit made. Cut to new-age businesses, where the KPI has become valuation. While as a founder, you can deliver scale, it is the investor who delivers the valuation. In your bid to run behind valuation, you tend to make two critical mistakes: one, you tend to think of the investor as someone above you in the food chain; and two, you lose sight of the fact that the story is between you and the customer. It is important to remember that the investor is just another vendor, only he deploys capital just as someone deploys technology or labour. *Aapne usko bhagwan bana liya hai*, you have given him a God-like status. This was a mistake I made, and you definitely need to avoid it. Of course, since we live in a capital-deficit economy, this thinking is that much harder to implement, but success lies in never losing sight of it.

3. Give Your Family a Seat at the Board—Do Not Go by the Western Concept of Arm's Length/Related Party

The way of life in Western, developed countries is that, as soon as the child turns eighteen, he is thrown out into the world to fend for himself. Of course, he is free to come home on vacations, where the parents will happily feed him, but that's all there is to it. You are financially separated. In India, though, our concept of family is entirely different, and the family occupies pride of place in our overall set-up. Cut to the business world and no marks for guessing that 99 per cent of profitable businesses in India are family-run. Think of traditional businesses and you are bound to think of Baniya businessmen who are known to work deeply as a family unit, while being true to their hisab-kitab. In the start-up world as well, the only profitable, bootstrapped businesses are run by brothers or by a husband–wife duo or a family. Just because your business has capital coming in from the US, you do not have to go by their concept of management—of not involving family in business.

To my mind, the concept of a related-party transaction in India is totally irrelevant. If I work with family, I will still give them the same rate as the market and will get the same deliverables. The added advantage that I may get is that a family member may work with me on a lower MOQ (minimum order quantity) or that they may take a credit risk on me. Being the capitalist economy that India is, everything in any case happens at arm's length here—after all, *dhanda, dhanda hai aur rishtedari, rishtedari*; business and relations can be handled separately with the same individual. You therefore need to be absolutely unapologetic about working with family.

Additionally, you need to remember that you don't need loyalty in good times—opportunity does the task. Loyalty is tested and needed in bad times. To expect loyalty from your employees or investors in bad times is to set yourself up for heartbreak. After all, people are simply driven by their next paycheck. That said, you have to be extremely careful in choosing the right people—something that I have highlighted throughout my story, where each of my wrong hires cost me dearly.

In bad times, the only people you will find standing beside you will be your family. You cannot even rely on your friends of twenty years—they may go completely silent on you. If you choose to work with your spouse, there should be no hesitation in designating them as co-founders as well as giving them a seat on the board, by virtue of their capability but also of the fact that they are invested in your success and will be the victims of your failure, like no one else.

4. Don't Be a Martyr to Your Own Cause: Founder Liquidity First

Put yourself first, always! As a founder, don't feel shy of liquidating your stock at every secondary sale opportunity. Cash in the bank will only make you bolder. Don't optimize for higher valuations in subsequent rounds. In fact, as a thumb rule, at least 80 per cent of the proceeds of any secondary sale should come to the founders. You may allocate the balance 20 per cent of secondary cash to ESOP holders and angel investors. It doesn't bode well to give any angel more than their original investment round in any secondary before the IPO. I've given more cash exits to my angels and ESOP holders than any other founder in India—not one person, however, was thankful enough to publicly stand by me. People made 80–250x returns, and bought homes and cars. I had to literally beg some angels to sell in earlier rounds—they were that greedy.

Also, make sure that all secondary sales can only happen through you—never make the mistake of letting them sell in the open market.

When it comes to your employees, do not offer them liquidity worth more than one year's salary or 50 per cent of their vested shares, whichever is lower.

Much as you work hard for your business, do not forget to ask investors for more shares whenever you deliver a milestone beyond their expectation to cover for your dilution! And last but not least, always plan for tax payout.

5. Beware of Certain Professions

Now here is a learning that I could come under fire for, but that cannot be reason enough for me to shy away from sharing it. In my experience, there are certain professions which suck value from you with nothing to show for it in return. At the extreme end of value-destroying professions are, in my opinion, drug peddling, prostitution and pimping, banking, journalism and legal professions. At their best, these professionals and professions offer you false comfort; they may even numb you momentarily, but fundamentally, if you spend disproportionate time on them, they will end up destroying you. You need to be extremely wary of them.

* * *

All that said, I would definitely encourage you to go ahead and build your own venture by all means, if you feel strongly enough about it. There isn't any reason why you should let the thought that you could make mistakes hold you back. My only advice would be, make sure these mistakes are new and not the ones that I fell prey to and paid a price for.

As for my story, love me or hate me, as long as you are not indifferent to the story and the many lessons it has to offer, I would consider myself successful in what I had set out to do by sharing my journey with you.